SPIRITS of SEDUCTION

free at last

KANDI ROSE

Spirits of Seduction
Free at Last

Copyright © 2010 by Kandi Rose

ISBN: 978-0-9766197-9-6

Spirits of Seduction
By: Kandi Rose

TABLE OF CONTENTS

Endorsements

Kandi Rose was a guest on my program, "In HIS Presence" on VTN. She has a powerful testimony of how God delivered her from an X-rated lifestyle to a G-rated. I am sure you would be blessed by reading her book, and I highly recommend it.

Jeanne Caldwell, Vice-president, Victory TV Network

I first met Kandi Rose when her call to VTN TV was transferred to my office several years ago. She was interested in sharing her testimony with our viewers in order to help those who may be struggling with addictions she had dealt with in her life. Kandi's testimony touched me in such a way that I felt it needed to be heard by men more than women. As she finished her story, I realized that she needed to document it so others, especially men, could read how the power of lust and drugs can rip your life apart. I could not help but suggest to Kandi that she write a book about her experiences, which she did. When I received it, I sat down and read it from cover to cover. Kandi eventually appeared on "In His Presence" to talk about her first book, and I am sure she will write many more, as she continues her walk with our Lord.

Dan Vukmirovich, Victory TV Network

Dedication

I want to first and foremost give all honor, praise and glory to my Lord and Savior, Jesus Christ. It was He who rescued me from the, Spirits of Seduction.

I want to dedicate, this book in part to my friend, Life Coach and Mentor, Evangelist Tracey Mitchell.

Special thanks to Pastor Mark Haston, Sr. Pastor of First Assembly of God, in Hot Springs, Arkansas for the many hours of editing the original version of this autobiography. To Pastor Jerry Hobbs, in acknowledgement for the many hours you invested editing the 2nd edition. To Charlotte Hansen, I cannot thank you enough for your precious time and the development of my new website.

This book is also dedicated to my late mom. She not only prayed for me, but also showed me true Christianity is a holy and loving lifestyle. When I faced a crisis I wanted what mom had, I wanted Jesus…Thanks mom for showing me the way!

Spirits of Seduction
By: Kandi Rose

Papa, you are my hero. My real dad never showed me the godly love of a true father ... you did. You Papa are a true picture and example of Christ's love.

Lil, you are my timid friend who had the courage and boldness to invite me to church. Thank you for your prayers and for your witness. You noticed a soul that needed Jesus, and recognized a heart that needed healing.

Finally, Brother John, you were the special evangelist that God used to preach the Gospel message... Thanks for obeying God and going to that little church. My life is forever changed.

Introduction

As you read this story, please be aware that I only want to bring glory to God. There is nothing glamorous about sin and devastation. It is, however, my story of God's amazing Grace.

I Timothy 4:1 Now the Spirit speaketh expressly, that in the latter times some shall depart from the faith, giving heed to seducing spirits, and doctrine of devils.

There are unseen forces of good and evil constantly at work trying to influence our choices. This battle begins as a small child and continues throughout our life. It is a battle between good and evil. We are told in John 10:10, that Satan is a thief who has come to steal, kill and destroy. Satan, the devil, is real. He is not some character with a pitchfork, but a spirit who leads many demons to influence the body, mind and soul of mortals.

The first seduction was by the serpent in the Garden of Eden. Throughout the Bible and right up to this present age, he has been promising false peace, joy and happiness. ***The word, seduce means to draw aside from right conduct or belief, to corrupt, to lead astray from chastity. Seduction means act of enticing from virtue by promises.***

When we hear the word ***seduce*** or ***seduction*** we generally think of sexual behavior. That portrait is not entirely true; the devil has various forms of seducing spirits. Even as an innocent child those spirits had free rein in my father, resulting in incest. Through the pages of this book my purpose is to

Spirits of Seduction
By: Kandi Rose

expose his tactics that would hinder us from having an intimate personal relationship with a Holy God who loves us.

I trust, this real life story, will enable you to evaluate your life; to determine if your life or the life of someone you love has fallen victim to seducing spirits.

Satan in his rebellion against God delights in continually trying to destroy the beautiful plan that God has for your life; attempting to replace them with lies of deception and destruction.

When Jesus died on the cross, He broke Satan's power over us. We have the power and ability to make the right choices, to turn from our sinful actions, and change wrong attitudes through repentance. Through Christ we can live a consistent Godly lifestyle, free from all seducing spirits.

May you discover the great joy and peace that emanates from knowing you belong to Jesus.

Note: Due to the sensitive nature of some of the material in this book, some of the names have been changed.

CHAPTER 1
Daddy's Demons

Oh, how I loved my daddy. Everyone who met daddy loved his personality. To neighbors and friends, he was thought of as a fine family man.

Our family *seemed* normal. We did normal family things; we went on outings, picnics, and special occasion activities. We appeared to be the average American family. My father worked everyday and arrived home in the early afternoon. I never saw daddy drunk, I cannot remember fights or violence in our home, but there was an evil spiritual force active in our daily lives.

I was a very affectionate, kindhearted little girl. My mother never had to spank me. I always wanted to please her and daddy. I was promoted in school three times when school curriculums were based on a six-month program of promotion instead of one year.

My mother taught me good morals and manners. I cannot remember being anything but obedient and doing my best to please my parents. I was a very innocent and naïve little girl. I had no idea that my family and I were victims of seducing spirits that would eventually destroy our home.

It is sad but true, there are evil forces that lurk behind the scenes of homes tearing lives apart and eventually leaving nothing but sad memories. As I reflect on my life, I am not only aware of these seducing spirits but also intensely aware of the Holy Spirit and angels that intervened on my behalf.

Spirits of Seduction
By: Kandi Rose

When I became an adult, my mom shared with me, that when she was pregnant with me, daddy had kicked her in the stomach so hard that it knocked her out of bed. On another occasion, when I was a baby crying in the crib, he slapped my tiny face. From that point forward, Mom vowed to never leave me alone with him; I do not remember her leaving me with anyone, not even family members. Little did she realize, that the deception of seducing spirits were active right under her nose. There is something very enticing about sin, something so evil, that the very idea of almost getting caught is exciting.

Innocence Stolen!

One of my earliest childhood memories is of daddy performing a sexual act on me. These horrendous acts began at the tender age of three would continue through my early teen years. Years later, I realized that the evil spirit of exhibitionism had become a major factor in my life.

My mother would, pray for me and taught me to pray the child's prayer, "Now I lay me down to sleep." Mom grew up as an adopted child to a very elderly, affluent family. They never expressed love for her and basically used her as a housekeeper. She never heard the tender words of love, affirmation or self-worth.

When my father, a migrant worker from Tennessee, came to pick cherries in upper Michigan, he instantly stole mom's heart. He was a likable, smooth talker who appeared to be 'the catch of a lifetime'. I am sure she dreamed of someone who would show her love and affection.

Spirits of Seduction
By: Kandi Rose

Mom grew up in church, but it was simply what people in their social class did, they went for appearance sake. From the outside in, her family had the appearance of what seemed good and moral. One of her brother-in-law's was a schoolteacher and principal. The other brother-in-law was a successful, affluent farmer and owner of vast cherry orchards. Both were avid church attendees. Yet these men allowed Satan to use seducing spirits to molest my mother.

Family Secrets

For the all the wrong people that mom would encounter, God sent someone who would change her life forever. That person would be her Sunday school teacher; she taught her that Jesus loved her. To a young woman, deprived of love, those words were wonderful to hear. That is why people who work with children and teens are very important in God's kingdom. Their influence has the power to change a life forever.

Mother had not experienced a true conversion with Christ, while I was growing up, but she had great respect for God. I remember that she told me about my body being the temple of God and that no one should touch it until you are married. She had no idea what was going on in secrecy.

Daddy had told me that if I told mom about his lascivious ways, she would have a heart attack and die. I had seen these attacks; she would turn blue and was unable to breathe. One can only imagine how scary this was to a child. I grew up living in dread that my precious mom would die and leave me. So I did not want to seal her fate by telling daddy's awful secrets.

Spirits of Seduction
By: Kandi Rose

When illicit sex is introduced to a child, teen, or adult it becomes an evil doorway for the demonic forces and addictions to step in. One act of sin will always leads to another. Since mom had taught me to pray I was aware of God. With that knowledge I started feeling guilty about what was going on.

I now understand that the guilt was not God, I was just an innocent child, a victim of seducing spirits. After praying, "I lay me down to sleep," under my breath I would always add, "Please forgive me God." I know now that there are countless millions who have been seduced and understand exactly what I am talking about. Perhaps you have lived in 'silent suffering' or maybe you are like me; I went from being abused to becoming the user.

To those who have had similar experiences, or perhaps you are still experiencing this awful demonic attack; let me assure you that Jesus loves you. There is a way of escape.

Touch Me No More

When I was eleven years old I remember hearing the older kids talk about sex. One day, when I got off the school bus and began walking down our country driveway, there stood daddy. He was off to the side, behind the shed, as usual exposing himself and grinning real big. I boldly proclaimed, "Daddy I'm a big girl now and you're not going to touch me anymore!" That had to have been the Holy Spirit to give me such boldness and to say it with such authority because I was always petite, meek and timid. He never touched my body after that. God must have put a fear in him that I just might tell. The indecent exposure, however, continued daily for the next five years.

Spirits of Seduction
By: Kandi Rose

I Had to Tell Someone

We eventually moved back to Chicago. It was a horrible time, and I grew to hate the sight of a man's naked body. Daddy even tried to give me money to show myself to him. One day, I had enough. I risked telling mom even with her health condition

Mom and I had always maintained a close relationship and I knew she loved me. She showered me with affection, playing games and spending fun filled times together. Mom always said that I was her gift from God. She had rheumatic fever when she was little and they said she would never walk again. After being bed-ridden for many years, God performed a miracle in her life and she walked. The doctors instructed her to avoid pregnancy as they thought it might kill her, so when I was born, it was yet another miracle. Mom treated me as a treasure.

At age fifteen, I gave her the news and it crushed her world. I told her all about daddy's evil abuse. I emotionally could not deal with it by myself anymore. Mom did not take the news well; she was so shocked, she had no clue. The enemy had been so deceptive. Mom cried and cried, then in a hateful fit of anger confronted daddy. He denied it; over and over he played the part more like a victim than the victimizer. He claimed that I was lying but mom knew better. She knew lying had never been a part of my character. Better yet, mom knew daddy's character because of what went on behind closed doors. His perfect father image was a facade. It was hard for her to conceive that he was evil enough to molest his only child. I respected and honored my mother for believing me. Millions of people are not believed when they reveal the dark secrets that have tormented them. Thank you, mom, for listening.

She immediately threatened divorce. With him crying and begging, I urged her to stay with him. He was still in denial and I could not bear the thought of them divorcing. Mom agreed to keep the marriage together because of my hysteria. But it was not long before he began exposing himself again.

Exposed

There was not a door leading to their bedroom, it was a little off set from the kitchen, separated only by a curtain. Mom was doing dishes at the sink and I was at the table. I turned and there he was with the curtain slightly parted exposing his self and grinning as usual. I stepped back into the small pantry and waited for mom to turn around. When she did I pointed to the bedroom doorway. She saw for herself and that sealed his doom.

Dad had many multiple addictions; anger management, as you can imagine, was not his strong suit. He threatened us with his army machete that he kept behind the front door. With our lives in danger, we left with only the items we could swiftly stuff in plastic bags.

We did not have a car and mom did not know how to drive. By using a city bus we moved to another neighborhood in Chicago, where she rented a 3-room apartment and walked miles to work at a cheap factory job. We left all our personal belongings behind just to escape daddy's demons.

After walking to and from a hot, tiresome job in the factory, she would sit in the dark crying for hours. A spirit of depression had seized my poor mom. For seventeen years she had been a kind, loving, and faithful wife. Now she felt that there was no hope.

A Tormenting Spirit

My mom remained kind and loving towards me, but other evil forces came upon her. The spirit of hate, bitterness and un-forgiveness entered our home. These are tormenting spirits from the pit of Hell that will eat away at your mind and emotional stability. Those spirits bound my precious mom until the day she became a born-again Christian and her heavenly counselor healed her broken heart.

As for me, even though I had kept loving daddy through my childhood, it was like my eyes were opened and I was filled with hate, bitterness, and un-forgiveness as well. Poor me, how could he have done that to me, his little girl? It was the beginning of Satan's negative voice that would follow me for years to come.

For nearly twenty years I followed lie's that led to destruction. During those years I led others astray through the spirits of seduction. It did not happen overnight, but little by little, compromise eroded my character. I rationalized, justified, and minimized my actions through my destructive choices. A spirit of self-pity set in; I blamed others for my condition, I was always making excuses, and saying, "poor me"!

If you had told me, at age fifteen, I would end up living such a shameful lifestyle, I would not have believed it. I was sweet and naïve and my life forever altered.

Spirits of Seduction
By: Kandi Rose

I weep for the teens and the youth of this world. That is one purpose for this book; to reveal to the younger generation that there is a spiritual battle consistently raging in your mind, heart and soul. It is the battle for your eternal souls.

Seduction means to be led astray, to entice, or to corrupt. Do not let the enemy take you down a path of heartbreak, filled with severe consequences. Do not permit the enemy to waste your precious life and ultimately send your soul to hell. There is a God who loves you and knows the heartaches you have already endured. Let him comfort you and heal your broken heart.

Allow God to be the love of your life, your best friend. Satan wants to destroy you emotionally and physically, but Jesus has great plans for your life. He wants to take all the bad and turn it for good, so you can show others that he is Alive! Your life can have meaning and purpose.

God created you with special talents and abilities so that you can help others find their way to joy and peace through Christ Jesus. As I look back, I see not only the evil spirit of hate and unforgiveness that oppressed me, but also the spirit of self-pity. Regretfully, I lived the next twenty years blaming others.

I challenge you to give your heart and life to Christ and allow Him to carry your burdens and give you a life that you have always dreamed about; a life of love, happiness and joy. Peace!

CHAPTER 2
A Victim of Rape

Prior to my mother's separation from dad, I made some choices that would leave scars on my life for many years. I became influenced by older teens in high school. The attacks of Satan were well orchestrated as he played them out in my life. The tactics of Satan are not new. He has been engaged in this type of warfare against God's children for generations.

Spirit of Rebellion

Everyone desires to be liked and accepted. Therefore, we often go along with the crowd and usually end up paying a great price for the choices we make. One day, a friend and I cut class, but the principal was right outside the door and caught us. We were told by the principle to bring our parents to school. We 'freaked out', hopped on an inner city bus and rode it to the end of its route.

That day we ransacked cars and stole a carton of cigarettes from a glove box. I mentioned I was a good girl but at the age of eleven I had started smoking cigarettes as a result of peer pressure.

By nightfall, we ended up in a very bad neighborhood and spent the night in a filthy, hallway. Fortunately, someone reported us to the police and they found us hidden in a dark, cold basement. Eventually, we were taken to the police station where our parents came to retrieve their 'little darlings'. We were fortunate that they found us alive and well.

Had it not been for the protection of God over our lives, we could have fallen into some very bad hands. Thank you Jesus!

Beware of Friends You Choose

My grades went from excellent to failing due to the class cutting. When I turned 16, I quit school. I was in the last half of my junior year when things went from bad to worse. During this time, I got involved in a gang. I started drinking wine in alleys, sniffing airplane glue from brown lunch bags, and getting into fights with rival gang members.

Actually, I was still very naïve. I heard that a girl was going to assault me. I remember being so terrified... I decided that I was no longer going to be the victim of someone else's abuse. When I saw that tall girl coming down the street with a mean look on her face, I took off my coat and I hit her first.

From that time on, I refused to live in fear of another's actions. I escaped the grip of fear only to be ensnared by a spirit of rage. Anger empowered me; it would become the fuel to a rage filled heart.

Of course, we know that fighting does not solve anything. God is our defense and reminds us that vengeance is His. This lesson would not be learned quickly and for the next twenty years I fought like a caged lion.

A few months later, we moved to another neighborhood, where it did not take long for Satan to come knocking with even worse temptations. At least I was away from the gang, but I kept making bad choices, which brought about harsh consequences.

Spirits of Seduction
By: Kandi Rose

My mother was heartbroken. She faithfully worked in the factory and lived a very lonely life. On top of her misery, my behavior made it worse. I was now letting that spirit of rebellion rule my heart and life. Mom was easy going and because I had been through so much she was hesitant to discipline me harshly. I had changed from Jekyll to Hyde. Now with my dad out of the picture I did whatever I felt like doing.

When there is no restraint or accountability to listen to authority, freedom will quickly enslave you. I became a slave to sin, as Satan began to use me. I went from being abused to being the abuser.

One Un-Ending Party

In this life, you will make a choice, a choice to live for either God or Satan to. Our lives and our choices we make affect those around us. Our lives influence each other either for good or evil. I pray this book will be instrumental in influencing you to live for God. It is an awesome, exciting way to live, partnering with God and showing others the way to life everlasting through Christ our Lord.

I eventually started drinking wine and whiskey; I smoked pot, and took a series of upper's and downers. I even tried cocaine and shot up with dioxin but had a bad experience while using these drugs. The night I shot up I must have had an over dose as the result was horrendous.

Although there were plenty of gangs in Chicago, there were none in my immediate neighborhood. Later on, I would associate with a well-known motorcycle gang. There were many of us who hung out on street corners, drinking and fighting between ourselves. We also met with teens from all over the Chicago area for illegal street drag races between the teens to see who had the fastest car. There was a particular street where many factories were located, where we would frequently race. The police would come; we would scatter, only to return the next night. It was one un-ending party scene.

Everything appears exciting and fun when you are young. It is addictive. Even later in life, I kept pursuing cheap thrills. Look around and you will see people of all ages caught up in seeking fun and excitement. The Bible says, "Sin is pleasurable for a season," that means a little while. It never thoroughly satisfies. You will always seek for more as you keep compromising your carnal side to obtain pleasure. Addictions of all kinds follow that obsession. You want to be accepted but overall you end up with consequences that bring great heartaches to not only you but also to your family.

I went to one party and got so drunk that I ended up being raped by several young men. Satan is out to destroy by whatever means possible. How pitiful and sad that we cannot see his motives beforehand!

That is why the Bible says to shun the very appearance of evil. Evil people can corrupt your language and compromise your morals. Choosing friends that love God will help keep you on the right path. This is where so many fall prey to destruction.

Victim of Date Rape

On another occasion, I went on a date with one of the most popular guys in the neighborhood. He was seventeen and I was sixteen. I was so excited because he appeared to be a real

Spirits of Seduction
By: Kandi Rose

catch, but he ended up using me. In a dark garage sitting in his 57 Chevy, he forced himself on me. I began crying loudly, feeling humiliated. Suddenly, I heard the car door open and his uncle who was middle aged took over while threatening my life.

Some people would probably say, "She deserved it." She was not a virgin anyway and should not have been there. No human being should be treated in that manner. My heart goes out to women who are beaten, battered and bruised. Many times they become prostitutes just like I was soon to be.

Little by little, my heart continued to harden. It seemed like all men were alike. Later in life I wanted to use them before they used me. I had a tendency to not trust anyone due to being raped, molested, and later kidnapped. When we lose trust in people, we often lose trust in God.

Now I understand and know that it is never God's fault when horrible things happen to you. We all have a freewill to do good or evil. Later in life, I would learn that I could use my own will to make evil choices, choices that not only hurt me but many others as well.

Today, I have replaced hatred for mercy. I was once a terrible sinner and needed forgiveness and mercy. Jesus said that if we do not forgive others, he would not forgive us. Sin is sin, no matter how big or small. It's all wickedness in the sight of God.

If Jesus can forgive those who nailed Him to a cross ... then I can forgive also.

Spirits of Seduction
By: Kandi Rose

Relationships From the Pit

I soon met a twenty five year old man from Arkansas. He was the first man with whom I had consensual sex. I was sixteen and he would be the first of many. He went back to Arkansas and quickly sent me a greyhound bus ticket, so I went to check it out.

I was a city slicker who looked at this sleepy little town and thought, no way ... I would be bored stiff. But I always loved the south because my daddy was from Tennessee and we had family in Missouri. At sixteen though, rural living was far too dull for me. Needless to say, I mailed the engagement ring back immediately.

Soon after that short relationship ended, I met another man. This time he was a twenty-three year old married man. I was almost seventeen and he brought lots of excitement into my life, so I thought. At this time I wasn't looking for marriage or commitment, just fun.

Through the years, I would find only temporary happiness and eventually end up feeling empty, used and abused. This particular man was only at his house during the day because nights and weekends we were together. I don't even remember feeling guilty for being with a married man. Why, because Satan can easily desensitize our conscience. My lifestyle was beginning to harden my heart.

We continued to see each other for about a year. He was a 'pool shark', and I had acquired a fake I.D He was one of the best pool players I had ever seen and he taught me how to play and at times I was his partner.

Obsession

At that time, women very seldom shot pool. So many people were willing to throw down big money thinking that they had a sure win. My boyfriend was so good that he made up for any of my weaknesses. As time went on, playing pool and gambling would become one of my greatest addictions and obsessions.

For the next 20 years, I could not even enjoy the game unless I could play for something, which mainly meant beer or money. If I walked into a bar and there was no pool table or no one shooting, I'd go to another. I bounced around to many bars all by myself, driven with this compulsion.

I walked in with such a chip on my shoulder that if you even looked at me funny I was ready to fight. At that time a game of pool was only a quarter and you could line your quarters on the table and count how many people were ahead of you. I was ready to fight anyone if they jumped my quarter. I saw many fights over a pool table.

Once, I saw my boyfriend beat someone terribly with a cue stick. It can quickly become a toxic situation when booze, pool and gambling were in the mix.

My boyfriend, with me in the car, frequently stole cars. Looking back I praise God we never got caught. Sooner or later the Bible says, "Your sin will find you out." So if you continue, no matter how slick you think you are, the crime eventually catches up with you. After about a year, I left this relationship only to end up in one worse waiting around the corner.

The self-pity and blame game were in full swing. The devil must have really been rejoicing as he continued to lie and deceive my thinking.

Do Not Tell Me What to Do

A spirit of rebellion will harden your heart. My attitude through life was much the same of millions of teens and adults. The attitude is, I will do what I want, when I want, and no one is going to tell me what to do, so do not try to change me! Often you will find many older people who act and talk that way, especially those who live bound in addictive behavior.

That is the basis of all domestic dysfunction and violent behavior. Each individual tries to be in control, while in all reality, they are already out of control. I am so glad that the Holy Spirit is in control of my life now.

That kindhearted, sweet, little girl had now transformed into a bitter, unforgiving, young woman. Roots of demonic forces came that bring great misery and destruction to any life.

Revenge will often seem justified when someone you love has been victimized. Hollywood has a way of glamorizing rage. Do not be fooled. Ask those who have been harden by a spirit of revenge, if it helped to heal their broken heart. It does not, it never will.

Murder in my Heart

Very late one evening, after drinking heavily, I started listening to the evil spirits taunting my mind. I took my friends knife and had him drive me to my dad's apartment. As I was walking up that dark stairway, to the second floor, hatred boiled up in my spirit in a way that I had never felt before.

I began beating furiously on daddy's door but with no response. Then, unexpectedly, he jumped out the door and threw me to the floor. I was drunk and he quickly overpowered me. I remember the knife narrowly missing my own throat. I could almost taste the metal as it went by my jugular. I was cursing and screaming loudly when my friend came up the stairs to check on me. Daddy, quickly, released me. Of course, he did not call the police. What would he say, "She's here to get revenge for the incest?"

Frustrated, I immediately began to develop a plan for a second murderous plot. Within a short time, I jammed a butcher knife down the waistband of my jeans, and once again, headed to my dad's apartment. This time he was not home, but a woman, likely a girlfriend, answered the door. I kicked the door all the way open, and boldly walked in without an invitation.

I had a demonic look on my face, a bad attitude and a mouth full of curse words. I began demanding any items that belonged to mom and I. Since it had been a while since we had departed dad's company, the woman said that daddy had thrown it all out the window in the back yard.

This infuriated me. I began looking throughout the house, and noticed a 3-D picture hanging on the wall that I had bought my mother by selling Christmas cards. I yanked it off the wall and turned to see a very frightened lady. This only encouraged me as I was enjoying the thrill of finally being in control. Ironically, the picture was of Jesus, who twenty years later would become the love of my life.

I am so grateful that my evil plot did not succeed. I would be on death row or already executed for murder. Often, we view those who are incarcerated from a self-righteous persuasion, when in truth; they are simply sad, broken and hurting people trying to escape the horrors of childhood.

Everyone is a Sinner

According to Isaiah 64:6, we are born with a sinful nature and our righteous morality is as a filthy rag. We need Jesus to take away our sinful nature, which includes our thoughts, actions, and attitudes. It is His Holy Spirit that comes into our hearts and makes us brand new and born again. (2 Cor. 5:17) He is an awesome and a wonderful God.

I escaped death many times. My friends and I would hang out on street corners and wait for someone to come and take us joy riding. We looked for someone that had both a car and accesses to alcohol or drugs. We would even jump in a total stranger's car just for thrills and so-called excitement.

Several times we narrowly escaped the police. They would pursue us, as we would dodge in and out of traffic on small two lane residential streets and alleyways.

On one occasion, a girl who was riding in front suddenly stiffened her leg and slammed her foot on top of the driver's foot onto the accelerator. We were on the congested expressway when I began slapping her face and tugging on her leg to get her foot off the accelerator. Talk about a wild ride! We just laughed it off, not knowing that God had sent His angels to watch over us.

Rescued from danger

One hot summer day, I recall almost overdosing on downers called "Christmas trees". I vaguely remember my mom begging me to stay home. Looking back now, I see how much grief and pain she suffered.

I was selfish ... I only thought about myself. On the day of my near overdose, it was approximately 90 degrees and I headed out to the streets wearing a heavy black leather jacket. I walked aimlessly not knowing where I was.

A stranger approached me and asked me if I wanted to go to a party. "Sure," I said. I was always interested in a party. Little did I know that rape was on his mind. I remember fleeing from his grasp and then running until I came to an apartment building. I ran up the stairway and pounded on a door until a young married couple opened the door. I told them a stranger was pursuing me so they let me in and the husband took me home.

I thanked him but I did not thank the Lord. I didn't know he was really the one behind my rescue. I'm thanking you now Lord.

It is man's nature to live with selfish motives. Without Christ living in our hearts, we become introverted focused on self. We neglect to recognize the hurt and needs all around us. I could have been a real comfort and blessing to my mom, instead, I became a thorn in her side. I was selfish and would waste years of my life pursuing, elusive happiness.

All I could think about was my pleasure. When my mother would ask me to stay home at night with her I would curse her relentlessly. Like a crazy person I would throw food, furniture and even scissors at her. However, when I came to know Christ, one of the first things I did was to beg my mom's forgiveness with true remorse.

I cried a river of tears over my sinned stained life and behavior, but my precious mother was so compassionate. She reminded me of what Jesus said on the cross, "Father, forgive them, they know not what they do." She bestowed the same grace upon my life, always showing me God's unconditional love.

CHAPTER 3
I Became Pornography

Mom was so lonely. I imagine as she walked to the corner store or restaurant she would hear the loud, country music and laughter pouring out of the local nightclub. These places appear to be so much fun. People are drawn in, looking for someone to talk to, longing for companionship.

The world is full of lonely people, seeking the need to belong to somebody or some group. That is why bars and gangs are so appealing. The devil has a counterfeit for true happiness, peace and pleasure.

While I was going through so many destructive consequences, the devil set a trap with which to ensnare my mother. Thankfully, not to the extreme I had experienced, but nonetheless seducing spirits sent my mom in the wrong direction.

Mom had loved country music but had never been one to partake of the nightlife scene. She was a good wife, a wonderful mother, and a homebody. I now know, it was her loneliness that would draw her into the club scene. Sadly, I was not there for her. She would sit every night crying in a darkened room. When she did start going to clubs, it quickly became an addiction.

Mother would sit and slowly sip vodka and orange juice all night. She never brought men home, but soon mom met the man she would marry. Mom did not realize it then but he was a gift from God to her.

He was a wonderful, caring man, who treated my mom with love and respect. He called her "angel" until the day she went to heaven. He became my gift from God as well. This was the first man to truly show me the love of Christ. He was a gift to us both. Of course, mother had a hard time believing he was for real, because trusting a man was difficult for her. She kept expecting him to change, but he did not. Both he and my mother would accept Christ years later and life became even better.

Prior to turning eighteen I met a man while working at a local factory. I was only employed there for a short time, but long enough to meet Carl. I thought I was in love with him and quickly moved into his parents home where he resided. We had very little in common except for our incessant desire to party. It did not take long before we would be unemployed, which only fueled our drinking binges.

Go-Go Dancer

Carl did not like to work; therefore, when a friend of mine told me about her job as a Go-Go dancer and the money she was making, I was interested. Let me explain a few details about the exotic scene. As ridiculous as it sounds, the go-go clubs were very alluring. To a party girl it appeared glamorous.

I was very excited about being able to make money. I had always lived impoverished and this looked like the opportunity of a lifetime. My friend drove me to her agent's office and I was immediately impressed. There were women ranging in ages from teens to fortyish. It was like a scene from the movies; the women were powdering, perfuming and primping in a large room filled with dressing tables. Colorful sequined lacey costumes hung everywhere and I could hardly wait to get to see how they would look on me. They were beautiful, colorful, Las Vegas style costumes. They were expensive and custom designed, but before it was over I would find out that all this was a cheap front and a farce. Satan exploits men and women through live pornography.

My first night on stage, fear gripped my heart. I quickly learned that if I closed my eyes while dancing, my inhibitions would leave. I loved to dance and would quickly develop my own 'customers'.

It was like a spirit would overtake me and I would blend in with the atmosphere. I now realize that it was an evil spirit, inspiring me. I became very creative. I was one of the best, in performing for the devil. Today, I am now part of the worship group at my church. How quickly, God can transform a life.

Magnetized by Money

The spirit of lust and greed quickly engulfed my life. I loved the life of pornography that I was living. A hard heart was needed for this job and the devil had prepared me well in advance. Money, money and more money was my game. I had been seduced and now I would seduce others. The love of money is indeed the root of all evil. If we are not careful, it becomes easy to compromise morals for money.

My agent had connections to nightclubs throughout Chicago, Old Town, Rush Street, and even as far away as Gary and Hammond, Indiana. He was paid an extravagant commission for each of the girls who danced within these clubs. He would drive and pick up the girls who had no transportation. We received a flat rate; paid out in cash each night, plus commission on all the drinks we could hustle from the customers.

We would perform a twenty to thirty minute routine on stage, and then mingle with the customers alluring them to spend their cash and rack up high tabs on their credit cards. In order to make a profit, you had to be a smooth talker and a good con artist. It was disgusting and was one of the most degrading things I willingly chose to do.

In the beginning, I hated manipulating men. The experienced dancers would argue that, "Hey, they are here to use us… it is a mutual interest..." My philosophy quickly became, 'take every penny you can squeeze from them'. Needless to say, I learned to talk and act the part in order to survive. Before it all ended, I counted at least thirty-three different clubs for which I performed.

At age eighteen and unmarried, I became pregnant while dancing in those exotic clubs by Carl. The fifth month of pregnancy was one of the darkest times of my life. I was kidnapped at knifepoint and felt that I would surely die.

Taken Hostage at Knifepoint

Since I was earning a fairly good income, Carl and I were able to get an apartment. Since, he did not like to work all our income came from my hard labor. When I was not dancing, we would go and hang out on street corners with our friends. It would become one of the most terrifying nights of my life, a night that I would not soon forget.

Recently, we had met a twenty-five year old guy named Paul. No one knew much about him or his background and he was new to the block. We were having fun conversing and drinking, when suddenly Paul flew into a rage over an incidental argument and beat a local homeless man to a bloody pulp. Nobody stopped the attack... No one would, that is one of the first rules you learn while living on the streets.

Sadly, I have seen throats slashed and people almost beaten to death. It was not unusual for that type of activity to go on regularly. We were with another couple our age and the girl was also five months pregnant. It was getting late and we did not want to be harassed by the police so we invited this couple and Paul back to our apartment.

The stereo was blasting and we were laughing when I heard sounds of crying coming from the bathroom. Taking a quick census, I noticed Paul and my girlfriend were not in the living room. Only Carl, the boyfriend of the girl and I were together. I thought this was strange so I knocked on the door and now heard muffled crying.

Rape

I was suddenly aware of what was happening and began to violently beat on the door, cursing Paul and demanding him to come out of the bathroom. A few minutes went by and out he came. He ran into the living room and ordered the boyfriend of the girl in the bathroom to hit the road. Being the coward that he was, he left.

Paul went back into the bathroom with the girl and locked the door. I was furious. I knew what it was like to be raped and since she was pregnant it was even worse. I banged harder and harder, cursing loudly. We had no phone to call for help and I presumed that I could handle the situation alone. Not so. Paul was under the stronghold of demonic spirits.

My boy friend Carl was 6' 2" and just slightly taller than Paul, but was no match for this older, more muscular man. Carl took a butcher knife from the kitchen for protection, but Paul took it away. Then he ordered Carl, my girlfriend, and I into the living room and ordered us to disrobe. I was violently cursing and my friend could not stop crying because of what she had just been through. We were both pregnant and this was so humiliating.

Suddenly, Carl jumped up from the couch and headed out the second floor back door. While Paul was preoccupied, we quickly put our clothes back on and ran for the front door. He beat me to the door, where he told my girlfriend to get lost and tightly grabbing my arm jerked me down the street, threatening me with that big butcher knife.

Sheer Terror

I was screaming, cursing, trying to get free of his grip but his threatening assured me that he was crazy enough to kill me. Eventually I quieted down and that is when I realized I was alone and in real danger. This feeling of terror overtook me. It was just he and I. Suddenly, I felt alone. I was barefoot as we went through alleys until we came to Paul's grandmother's house. He did not let his grandmother see the knife he was holding, but I knew it was there, so I did as he said. He was at grandma's house to get money. ... I look back now and know that I was not alone; the God of heaven and earth was there with me. Had it not been for God that night I would not have survived that dark night

My boyfriend Carl had called the police and when Paul realized the police were there, he opened the second floor window and made me get out onto the roof of the next apartment building. It had a large overhang that was very sloping with about three feet between the roofs. With our hands extended on his grandma's house and our feet on the building next door we were able to suspend ourselves. Looking down made me know that with one wrong move it would all be over.

Rescued

I kept quiet not saying a word. One of the police officers noticed the screen was off this closed window and quickly figured it out. He pulled his gun out and ordered us to get inside. What a relief! I had grown up hating the police but tonight, I was thankful.

Evil had entered my life as an innocent child, now through my choices as an adult; I had created a place for evil to reside. Without doubt, I know that God was ever present and watching over my life or things could have turned out much different.

I still refused to change my lifestyle and things only grew worse. Later we would discover that this was not Paul's first encounter with violence. He was a sin sick man, who got his thrills by raping women with their boyfriend or husband present. He had done this many times before using knives or guns and beating the men when they protested.

Some years later, I was listening to the radio and heard Paul and his brother had been caught and convicted of murdering an actor in California. They were both facing the electric chair. I was not surprised, my hard heart rejoiced over his impending death. I feel shame now for feeling that way and hope that he had an opportunity to give his life to Christ before he died.

Death - Everywhere

Death seemed to be stalking me around every corner. My girl friend Marilyn, a dancer, picked me up one day in her boyfriend's T-Bird. We bought a gallon of Morgan David wine to go along with the whiskey we were drinking. It was 2:00 A.M. when another car with two guys pulled up beside us on Cicero Avenue. They wanted to drag race and we accommodated them. Cicero is a four-lane city street in Chicago and when the light turned green we roared away.

We were winning when the next light turned red with traffic coming from the other direction. Marilyn slammed on the brakes and slid into a U-Turn. We ended up front bumper to front bumper with the guys we were racing. It was a miracle no one was hurt except our vehicles. Instead of praising God, we became angry that our wine was gone. It had exploded all over us and it looked like we were covered with blood. We were cursing loudly because she knew her boyfriend was going to be upset. We never stopped to think we could have been killed or could have taken the life of innocent people. A year later, my friend Marilyn went to Tennessee to visit some friends and she along with another girl were killed when their car hit a tree. She was decapitated in the accident while speeding and drinking. She was only nineteen, how awful!

The devil has come to kill, steal and destroy and he has done a thorough job of destroying so many lives physically, emotionally and spiritually.

The work of the enemy's hand is evidenced everywhere. Through the years, so many of our street corner or bar friends have died through an overdose, an accident or murder. Others have ended up in jail or on death row. Although, I have been arrested numerous times I was never convicted or did time. That's a miracle in itself.

Car Theft

Carl and I were together for about a year and a half. He refused to work and never owned a car. He got his so-called thrills from stealing cars and taking them out joy riding. He did not try to sell the cars or strip off the parts that would have been too much work. He just drove them while he was drunk and eventually, would get caught. Carl parked one of these stolen vehicles overnight in front of our apartment and I took it to another neighborhood, not realizing I could have been caught and sent to prison.

Many women are in jail because of association with a man who influenced them for evil. Of course many men are in jail because of their bad choices with women. If I knew then what I know now, about the Lord, the entire course of my life would have been so different and I have enjoyed a much happier life. That is why I am passionate about sharing His Word with today's generation. I get so excited seeing God raise up young men and women who make a lifetime commitment to live under the protective care and watchful eye of the Lord. They are taking a stand for holiness; to live a "Godly" life, refusing seducing spirits to enter and control their lives.

Sin, the Source of Suffering

Carl, like so many suffered much pain and anguish from his wrong choices. One night, Carl stole a car and took it across two state lines, making the crime a Federal offense. He was

35

caught and served three years in a Kentucky state prison. He departed for prison three days before our daughter was born. My pretty little girl, what a precious gift she was from God.

I never recognized my baby girl as a gift from God. The devil blinds us to our blessings and keeps us from a life that has fulfillment, peace and joy. More self-pity set in as feelings of abandonment came during the birth of my daughter.

I was so blessed to have a mother who was there for me during these difficult days that were filled with heartaches and trials. The Bible tells us that we have a God, who when we come to the end of our selves, when materialism has vanished, and others have forsaken us, that He remains. He cares when no one else will. He promises, "I will never leave you or forsake you." Today, if you are feeling lonely or isolated, Jesus is there with you.

My life was devastated, emotionally broken and would spend many hours crying. Mother allowed my baby and me to move in with her and that was a comfort. Carl and I wrote each other everyday, with me promising to wait until he could get out. Three years seemed to be an eternity. He was hurting and I was wounded. As usual, I began to think only about myself and felt like I was left without hope and a dismal future.

Fuel on the Fire

Carl and I had a crazy relationship. I can only imagine what would have become of us had we lived out our lives together. Both he and I drank heavily, had real bad tempers and were constantly cussing and fighting.

There were wild neighborhoods in Chicago and I seem to feed on violence, which meant that I did not have the good sense to be afraid. Carl would often try to leave the bars after it got late, but I would persuade him to stay for just one more game of pool. I was addicted to gambling on the pool table. It would become a downfall in my life for many years.

Carl was jealous and now I realize why. I enjoyed all the attention I got from men. When I walked in somewhere I enjoyed the stares. I was a flirt and my hardened heart had produced a desire for enjoying being in control. Looking back I really cannot blame others for my wrong choices. Although I had been a victim of men's evil choices, I would make many evil choices, victimizing not only myself but also those I loved.

The Bible that says, "I will give you a new heart, I will take your stoney heart of sin and give you a new heart of love." (Ez.36:26) I hated the bad attitudes, the anger and negative emotions that were trapped deep inside of me. Today, when a bad attitude pops up, I ask God to give me an attitude adjustment. I do not carry bad feelings around that ultimately lead to destructive choices.

Tattoo Party!

One night, before Carl went to jail, we were at a party where almost everyone got homemade tattoos. They were made from India ink, needles and thread. I had Carl's initials put on my back, each letter of my name put on the fingers of my right hand and a dagger put on the top of my right hand.

I myself put the letters of Carl's name on my left fingers and a tattoo of a cross on my forearm. At the time, I did not realize what a cross really stood for. A cross is the symbol of the grace and mercy of Jesus... and that through His love we can have a new life.

Jesus offers us a life without guilt and shame. Strangely, no one had shared that with me. Four years after Carl had been released from prison; his best friend would put a gun to his head and would murder him over drugs. He had accused him of snitching to the cops. Sadly I remember his funeral, it reminds me that sin has lasting and eternal consequences.

While these events were devastating, I would soon go from the 'frying pan into the fire' with more destructive choices.

CHAPTER 4
A Cheating Heart

From the frying pan into the fire is an understatement. In looking back, I realize that every bad situation of my life was fueled by horrible choices. When my little girl was one month old I started leaving her with my mom while I hit the bars every night. I felt abandoned and alone and each night found me looking for love in all the wrong places and faces. Peter was a part-time drummer who I met in a bar on one of these occasions. He was good looking and a smooth talker. At the time he did not have a regular job either. Here we go again!

Almost immediately I moved in with him, his mom, his sister and her boyfriend. Mom would not let me take my baby to their house and her wisdom was right on. I started dancing again because no one in the house was working. I was given a business card by one of the customers at one of those clubs. He was a photographer and I was excited. In my foolish imagination I envisioned fame and fortune in posing for magazines as a model.

When I walked into his studio I was very impressed and it appeared much like one would have seen in the movies. There were huge and expansive colorful backdrops of gorgeous scenes with cameras everywhere and lots of bright lights.

The photographer had instructed me to bring a bikini and a towel since the first shoot was a scene with a beautiful ocean background with various shades of blue. It was so exciting!

More Deception

Needless to say, this situation did not turn out to be what I had hoped it would be. This photo session was a pretense, as this was complete nude modeling. This man wanted to exploit and use me and that is exactly what I allowed him to do. Money, money, money!

No need to Compromise

Again, so much of Satan's seducing spirits is deceptive and we become convinced that we must do whatever it takes to survive in this perceived dog eat dog world. Many people compromise their values when making career choices to enable them to attain not only enough money to survive but to obtain material possessions as well. You must remember, you do not have to compromise your faith and morals to get your daily needs met.

Christ Jesus is our provider. (Phil. 4: 19) He makes opportunities arise to meet our needs and nothing is coincidental or luck. The next time you get in a jam, ask God to help you and do not try to do it your way. You will be amazed how He always comes through for your life.

It is said that God is never late, but in fact, God always comes through many times it seems, like a last minute reprieve. He does this to strengthen and test our faith. Your faith will grow by leaps and bounds as you witness the power of this unseen God meeting your needs. He is indeed an awesome God.

When this so called modeling session was over, I felt so degraded. I have no idea what nasty magazines those photos went into. At the time all I was interested in was making a lot of money and was thrilled to do whatever it took to survive. That shoot became one of many sessions that would follow through the years and like dancing, it provided me with quick money.

The two and one-half years I was with Peter left memories of much heartache. He thought he was God's gift to women and of course my attitude was not any better. God made man to be with only one woman and vice versa

Wanting to be Loved and Desired

Even Christians have to be alert to the evil spirits of wanting to be desired, and to be found attractive, wanting others to notice the value of our talents and gifting. It may be difficult to wrap your mind around but God can literally meet those types of desires. He values us, desires a relationship with us, and has given us talents to be used for Him.

Some go so far as to justify becoming immoral because of this evil obsession, to be needed and loved. That type of destructive choice not only ends up destroying you, but will also devastate others as well. It usually starts out seemingly innocent with flattery and admiration. Proverbs 6 & 7 provides a warning of smooth talking people. I have been on both ends of that spectrum; I have been cheated on and I have been the cheater.

Along with flattery comes empathy for what you are going through, such as your wife or girlfriend not meeting your needs and causing you unbearable pain. Then the other party consoles you with a hug, which may begin with joking around, teasing, trying to get the other in a good mood.

Flee Flattery!

Spirits of Seduction
By: Kandi Rose

If you see these signs, get up and out. Do not spend time alone with the opposite sex when you are in such a frame of mind or the spirit of lust will rear its ugly head. It is devastating not only for you but your precious loved one that God gave to you.

When God said to not have sex outside of marriage, fornication, or adultery, having sex with someone other than your spouse, he knew it was for our own good. You can be sure that heartaches from such behavior can be spared when we follow God's way.

The spirit of lust comes at first as a thought. A thought that is dwelt on, if given an opportunity can eventually become a habit. This spirit of lust can initially come through someone showing unusual interest in you, a picture in a magazine or an Internet site. Music can even become a channel that can feed this spirit of lust. That is why it is very important that you monitor what you feed your mind and heart.

The devil will make a way for you to put those thoughts into action. Looking back, I now see that is what Satan used to imprison my mind and feelings. Once you open the door for sin, you have opened the floodgates of temptation and it will eventually enslave your mortal being.

At first, it brings pleasure and excitement, but it quickly leads to low self-esteem, guilt and shame. When you surrender to illicit sex, the end is predictable and you will end up feeling used and will cause you to use others as well.

I can only wish that I had known then what I know now. All of life is a spiritual battle and we need God's Spirit within us so we can say no to the urgings of the seducing spirits. The world is looking for love in all the wrong places and faces. It is only found in God. God is love and unbeknown to me, He actually loved me first while I was yet a sinner.

Five months after meeting Peter I became pregnant with my second child. A big blue eyed baby boy. Again I did not realize as I do now what a wonderful gift children are to our life. The Bible states, "God formed all of us when we were yet in our mother's womb." (Psalm 139) Therefore, there is no such thing as an accident and we are all born with a divine purpose and plan.

Children are a Blessing not Burden

We were created for God's pleasure. (Rev. 4:11) God gave us children to enjoy, but unfortunately many feel that their children are more of a burden than a blessing. I did not realize the extent of the blessings that can come through our children. I was always looking for fulfillment in people, places and careers.

I have always loved my children, but through the years they spent a lot of time in the care of babysitters and family members. How sad! Fulfillment comes from having a pure and personal relationship with God and then enjoying the family he's given us.

During my pregnancy, I suspected Peter was cheating on me. My best friend and him would tease and laugh with each other excessively. Also Peter would go out in the evening and come back all hours of the night. He did not have a regular job; therefore I knew he had to be up to something.

One of his best friends told me he was sleeping with my best friend. I would get in my car with my bottle of booze and ride around Chicago trying to catch them together. It always brought about a sickening feeling in the pit of my stomach.

Any of you who have gone through the cheating scenario know what it is like. One evening I saw them in a car and in my crazy, jealous rage I tried to run them over. I rammed their bumper several times but they escaped in the traffic.

I got hired as a cab driver and used to drive all over Chicago in it looking for them. When life gets this bad and the burdens get this heavy, you can become capable of doing some crazy things. One night I got so drunk that I kept the cab out overnight and lost my job.

I was eaten up with a jealous spirit and a heart filled with red-hot hatred. This was during my pregnancy, so when my baby was born and only three weeks old, I headed out for my best friend's house.

Vengeance, not the Answer

A big party was going on. I had hitch hiked a ride with a stranger to her house. I went to her back door and demanded she come out. I told her in my angry and cursing way that I was going to whip her. She came out along with everyone at the party and while I was alone, I was fearless. I was so full of hate and wanted revenge.

It was February and there was about a foot of snow on the ground. I punched her and down we went in the snow, putting her in a headlock. She had a handful of my hair and her finger inside my mouth, jabbing it. The neighbors called the police and when we heard sirens everyone starting yanking us apart and scattered back into the house.

The only part I can laugh about is that unbeknown to the people at the party; I had run inside the house also and hid in her closet. I could hear the police asking questions about me. Then I heard a snickering sound and realized one of Peter's friends was in the closet also. He had a good reason for hiding there, he was a wanted man and he was running from an arrest warrant.

After the police left, I came out of the closet and my sudden appearance freaked everyone out. I guess they had thought that the troublemaker was long gone.

I remember feeling so empty and numb. Revenge had not made me feel any better. Even if I had killed her I realized getting even does not make you feel better. Peter had left when I first showed up and of course I allowed him to smooth talk me again. He continued to cheat on me with not only my once best friend, but many others as well.

My life was one big temper tantrum, brought on by my drinking and unstable emotional state. Throwing baby food jars and other glass items at him was a common occurrence. I would cuss him relentlessly and we would fight like cats and dogs.

Temper Fueled by Jealousy

When your heart and mind is filled with hatred and contempt, you can and will do some very stupid things. One night while he slept I tried burning his black leather motorcycle jacket in our living room. See, I told you I could be quite stupid when the devil was in control of my thoughts. He woke up, put out the fire, and the fight was on.

For some strange reason, Peter was a little afraid of me. I can only think that his reason for fearing me was that he knew I was crazy enough to try anything. I was always threatening to kill him in his sleep with a butcher knife.

I had a raging temper fueled by jealousy and revenge that was always part of my character. Sadly enough when that jealously and revenge was induced by alcohol, I was totally unreasonable.

When I remember the many wasted years of my youth, I can only cringe. I was so influenced by seducing spirits that I felt like I was losing my mind at times. This type of lifestyle is not unusual in the world. The devil has been at work for thousands of years destroying people's lives.

Since Peter wasn't working during this time period I resorted to dancing again to make quick money. It was through the clientele of these nightclubs that I was able to meet wealthy businessmen. These men would become my "sugar daddies."

Sugar Daddies

These men offered big money for prostitution, and even more money was paid out for my dancing. They would get a room in big fancy hotels with champagne and food. They all drove Cadillac's or Lincolns and I was so impressed, at least in the beginning.

Spirits of Seduction
By: Kandi Rose

To console and justify my behavior, I would tell myself, "Peter's cheating on me, so why not?" A hard heart is a must if you want to survive in this business and an attitude that says if you try and use me, I am going to use you as well. So I became a cheater also. It is a sad admission, but my life was filled with these three temptations: dancing, modeling, and sugar daddies.

This activity would be part of my life off and on until I was thirty-five years of age. That is when Christ came into my heart and life and I was saved.

Three months after my baby boy was born I became pregnant with my third child, a beautiful baby girl. Now Peter happened to be at home when our son was born because it was in the afternoon. When my baby girl was born it was 5:30 AM and he was out and about as usual. My precious mom and wonderful step dad were there for me as usual. I thank God for their love and faithfulness to me. The Lord was there also but I did not know it.

I reasoned that surely two babies would want to make Peter change. He was so proud of them and I know he loved them but there was a spiritual battle raging within him as there was in me.

My second daughter was only 364 days younger than her brother. My oldest daughter was only two years and three months old when this precious third child was born.

The American dream life was about to happen for the children and me. However, without God as a single priority in our lives, the home wreckers would bring destruction to everyone.

When my third child was three weeks old I discovered a whole new life. I was twenty-one years old, had a cheating, unemployed boyfriend and our lives were filled with ongoing domestic violence mixed with alcoholism. I was broke, with no one to love and care for the four of us.

Prince Charming

There was a knock on the door and when I opened the door there stood a nice looking young man looking for Peter. This guy was clean cut and had recently come home from Vietnam. I invited him in and offered him a beer.

This stranger showed great interest in the kids as he held and played with them. I was overjoyed to see someone so attentive to the kids because Peter was hardly ever at home. I would wash and iron his clothes, tell him how nice he looked and off he would go into the arms of someone else. Yes, it was a sad situation, but when you're in love you will put up with a lot of unnecessary heartache. Unless you've been in a similar situation, it is hard to comprehend the craziness of it all.

There were many times in my life that I wondered how someone could put up with that kind of behavior from a man. I would often say about others, "I would never put up with that." Later in life I found find myself doing exactly what I said I would not tolerate. The Bible says not to judge others, but to pray for them.

CHAPTER 5
The Home wreckers

We all, Christian and non-Christian alike, have troubles. We are in a spiritual battle. When you commit your life to him and receive His Holy Spirit, it is then we find the strength needed to overcome those seducing spirits. Of course at this point in time I did not know what I know now.

I am so glad Jesus loved me enough to knock on my heart and I am also glad I let Him in. (Revelation 3:20) I am so glad that I did not refuse his voice of love, and shut Him out anymore.

Sadly though, I did not have the Holy Spirit living in me when Roy kept coming to the apartment and asking for Peter. I soon realized he had a great interest in me and I loved the attention he showered on me. He was a gentleman. He was not pushy, but kind and considerate. He was not at all like other men I had met. I was also infatuated by the fact that he brought food and beer with him when came to visit. He had a job. Wow, a real job! He was a tradesman, a pipe fitter in the union. He drove a new car and had no children or had ever been married. He had just turned twenty-one and this was all too good to be true.

In a short period of time Roy and I were deeply involved and when Peter found out about Roy he wanted to kill us. The cheater was mad he was getting cheated on. When we heard that Peter had a gun, we quickly packed up what belongings I owned and I moved in with Roy. He wanted not only me but my three babies as well.

Peter's wrath did not last long and shortly afterwards he married my best friend, which I felt was just a payback. I heard later that he kept cheating on her and would beat her worse than he beat me. At that time in my life I loved juicy news and laughed and said, "She wanted what I had and she got it, maybe even worse." The spirit of hate was still oppressing me.

The American Dream?

I could not believe the wonderful change Roy brought into my life. He also told me he did not want me to go-go dance anymore. He had a good job and I could stay at home while he took care of us. Wow! This was a first. He genuinely loved us. Crying babies and dirty diapers did not faze him a bit. I admit that I was still in love with Peter and was for some time. As each day passed, my love grew stronger for Roy.

After becoming a Christian I could see the similarities of marriage with our relationship with the Lord. When you first make a commitment to love, honor and obey God, a great love is not generally understood or heartfelt. As you begin to learn the character of God and notice His acts of kindness in your life, you cannot help but fall in love with Him. It is a love that grows with each passing day.

That is exactly what happened with Roy. As he showed his love by continual acts of kindness, I begin to realize that he was a wonderful person ... and maybe he would be my husband someday. After living together for about a year Roy finally asked me to marry him. I wore a white dress, had a nice set of wedding rings and was married in a little church. It is a sad thing to go through all the formalities of marrying someone you love, yet know in your heart that something is wrong.

Havoc to a Happy Home

We were not aware of the reason and truthfully; most people experience this same feeling. The missing ingredient was God. The only time His name was mentioned in our home was when His holy name was called in vain. He was not invited into our home, our hearts or our marriage. God was not placed first in our lives, so in time, Satan would bring havoc to this happy home. Oh how those seducing spirits love being a home wrecker!

Remember, we are in a spiritual battle! Satan does not like unity and when he sees two people united as one, he sets out to destroy that unity. One has only to look at the divorce rate, even among Christians. After you are saved you must maintain your commitment and never allow that love relationship between you and Christ Jesus suffer from inattention. That holy commitment is maintained through a strict spiritual disciplined life of righteousness. Going to church, reading your Bible, sharing your faith, and praying are needed for not only your personal strength, but will work for your marriage as well.

We seldom know what happened or went wrong at the time when our marriages fall apart. We question, how did this dream marriage fall apart? You can be assured it did not happen overnight. When married life begins to spin out of control, it is possible that the couple has lost control of their actions and behavior. It is even possible that affections and desires were literally taken over by seducing spirits. Remember, it is a spiritual battle (Ephesians 6:12) and there are evil spirits at work to destroy you. The devil is a home wrecker and he offers many types of temptations. If we choose to allow the temptations of Satan to exist in our life, we will suffer the destructive consequences. He not only wrecks our own life but our spouses,

children, family members and all others who are influenced by
our lifestyle.

Roy and I both went into the marriage as drinkers and I
definitely allowed this temptation take me way past being an
occasional drinker. I was soon out of control, unmanageable and
alcoholic. I either could not or would not admit this until years
later after our home was destroyed. Alcoholism is a home
wrecker and for those who have been there, done that, you know
the consequences and devastation it brings to bear.

I never admitted to having a problem, I would only admit
to being a social drinker. As a teenager I always bowed to peer
pressure. Later I played the blame game from the early days of
incest in my life to many wasted years in my adulthood.

Addiction

I always minimized and justified my drinking by telling
myself, you do not drink every day, all day from morning, noon
till night like those you see lying in the streets of Chicago. I felt
drinking on weekends with my husband was a good pass time
event. I was in much deeper into the drinking thing than Roy.
When we were out and Roy tired of the partying, he simply
wanted to go home; and did. I was never ready to go home if
there was a pool table in the bar and I could make a bet.

Gambling is another home wrecking device. Roy and I
would fight like cats and dogs over my drinking and gambling
because I was not ready to quit! I also rationalized why I drank
and I had a million excuses that included bills we owed, kids,
stress, etc. Whether its alcohol or drugs, the bottom line is that
there does not have to be an excuse. It is our choice. When Jesus

reveals Himself to us, it is up to us to choose Him because He gives us the power to be faithful to that choice.

I had a likeable personality but when I was drinking, I put on beer and shot "muscles." I thought I was tough. When irritations would build up, I would just explode. That may be the reason I ended up in harm's way so many times. I had a potty mouth that spilled out four letter words like a river, even in normal conversation. I did not have to be angry.

Provoking Domestic Violence

I was petite but proudly boasted, "dynamite comes in small packages." Of course, so does rat poison, but I never thought about that at the time. I would get right up in Roy's face and dare him to hit me, all the while cursing fiercely. He would push me away to get me out of his face and I would just get in his face again. It did not take long for things to get out of control. The four kids would wake up to hear and see this ugly scene. How horrible for them.

Needless to say, I became a huge thorn in my husband's side when under these evil influences. Now I can understand why they call drinking or drugging, "under the influence." It is without a doubt, an evil seducing spirit. Thanks to God, I am under a different kind of influence now, a Godly influence, the influence of the Holy Spirit. Jesus died to break Satan's power and influence over our lives. He came to set us free so that we could be all that He created us to be. There is power in the shed blood of Calvary! I am living proof to this day!

All we have to do is:

1. Confess I am a sinner and cannot change myself.
2. Believe only Jesus can change me and ask Him to save me.
3. Make a choice to live for God with all of my heart and turn away from all of my old ways.

Be willing to give Him your sins no matter how big or small they may be; "For all have sinned" in some way or another. He will then give you a new life (2 Cor. 5:17) and you too can live a godly lifestyle. Sadly though, I did not either understand or receive this truth until more wasted years had passed. That's why I am so compelled to share these testimonies with you.

Beneath the outward appearance of your life, is a wonderful human being that God created. You are precious and valuable to Him. I deeply desire to share my testimony with you and others, so everyone can be spared some of the heartache and destruction I have experienced. Deception always makes the grass look greener on the other side.

The Old Testament is full of actual accounts of godly men and women who sinned. When they repented and did a u-turn, God used their lives. Their stories are true and placed there for us to learn from their example and not go there! All that glitters is not gold; sometimes it's fool's gold. It is simply an imitation compared to the life God wants to give you if you will live for Him.

Pauper to Princess

After Roy and I were married we moved into a ranch style house with four bedrooms and a full basement. I could not

Spirits of Seduction
By: Kandi Rose

believe that this was happening to me. Me! We moved from Chicago to the suburbs, fifty miles north to a better environment to raise our children. I was used to dumpy apartments that came with so many cockroaches you would wake up with them crawling over you. I have eaten my share of pinto beans, macaroni and cheese and peanut butter. Now, I found myself blessed with a life that was a far cry from what it used to be.

A brand new home! Wow! And I was even able to pick out the colors for the carpet, paint, tile, etc. What an experience! It would not take long however, before the home wrecking spirit would come and destroy this happy home. There are some things you cannot blame the devil for, even though he is the evil spirit of influence behind the destruction. God gave us a free will to make choices. When those choices come before you, there is a battle that you will face in making the right choice.

The songwriter said it well, "I once was blind but now I see." The devil blinds our eyes to the truth and not until Jesus comes with the good news through a messenger do we understand the truth. I am one of his many messengers and you can be one also, if you are not already. I was so spiritually blind at the time. I would continually wreck our happy home with many addictions. Today, I have taken personal responsibility for my own choices and quit blaming everything and everybody. Yes, I was influenced by seducing spirits, but now I know the truth and that truth has set me free! Free to make Godly choices.

I soon became pregnant with my fourth child, a precious little girl. This would be Roy's only child. He was such a good daddy to all the kids and showed no partiality. Roy wanted to adopt the other three. He wanted them all to have his last name so we could all feel more like family. There are not many men willing to commit to this type of love.

Gambling Addict

Gambling was another home wrecker! Yes, I was a gambling fool when it came to shooting pool. I would play for money or booze; it didn't matter because gambling had become a very destructive obsession. Everybody likes to win. When we play a game, whether it's sports, cards or whatever, we like the idea of winning. That concept is not wrong as long as it is not for money and you learn to not be angry or depressed when you lose. Playing for money can get out of hand. Addiction to gambling or any other destructive habit can bring about wreckage and ruin in your personal life as well as your home.

This obsession becomes a driving force that compels one to keep indulging. My obsession took on other forms of gambling besides the pool table that included bingo, poker, horse races, etc. No one purposely sets out to become addicted to anything but, as we all know, if you give the devil an inch he will take a mile. My girlfriend told me, "Kandi, when you lived for the devil you lived for him good and when you live for God, you live for Him good."

I had a best friend from Chicago who also moved to the suburbs. Her name is Dorothy who I named my youngest daughter after. She is married with sons and at the time was about the same age as my children. Dorothy's life was not as crazy as mine. My crazy life came from some bad choices I had made as a teenager. God had given Dorothy a wonderful hardworking man for a husband.

They had purchased a new home as well. We lived close to each other and soon we were coffee clutching with lots of other neighbors. I would have as many as twelve ladies over almost every day. Since I had the most kids, the women would come to my house. I had four children in four and a half years span. When the youngest was born, the oldest was not even in kindergarten until five months later. I was indeed barefoot and pregnant! At the moment, life seemed so normal. I spent too time watching the soap operas and became very discontent with what I thought was a boring life. It is true, what you watch, read or listen to will affect your choices.

Bills, Bills! The Fight is on!

I met wonderful friends and neighbors who although were unlike me, they accepted and loved me. We would play poker during the day starting out with penny ante and going to dollar ante. I would cut corners on my groceries so that I could have more money to gamble. It became expensive to play. I started going to Bingo one night a week and eventually played 4 to 5 times a week. It was very costly in more ways than one. Roy made good money, probably more than some of our neighbors.

Spending cash and using credit cards, seemed the American way of life. Soon my gambling habit spiraled out of control and we were in debt. We were constantly fighting because there was never enough money to pay all the bills we had acquired. The big paycheck became too small and was never big enough. Debt is a home wrecker caused by our appetite for more material things. It is not worth losing your marriage for things. Things have no lasting value like your family and loving relationships.

My friends and neighbors did not lose control like me. I was the only one drinking during the day while we played cards. I was the only one drinking during Bingo. I was the wild one of the bunch and unknowingly provided my friends with something to laugh at, me. I quickly became the life of the party. I could tell the nastiest jokes, using horrible language.

Roy and I would throw big booze parties around our bar and pool table in our basement. Lots of couples would come, but everyone would not get as crazy as me. After a few drinks they would go home, but I could keep on drinking... drinking ... and drinking. I would plead for Roy to get a babysitter so we could go to the bar and shoot pool and of course gamble. Roy and I had many fights at a bar because I did not want to go home. I was obsessed! I craved the game as much as the alcohol.

I loved my children and thought I was being a good mom. I would play kid board games with them, take them to the beach, and go on outings and school field trips. Still I fell short in many areas as a good mother. It is so sad to know that I cannot turn back the clock and be the "Godly" mom that they so desperately needed.

Kids Suffered from my Choices!

I cussed my kids when they did not behave. Then I would spank them when they cussed. I never actually beat them physically, but emotional stress is just as damaging. I used babysitters a lot so I could selfishly go have a good time. I thought because I never left them alone that I was a good mom. I drank in front of them and later when they were in their teens I smoked pot with them. They heard my screams and cursing as Roy and I fought all hours of the night, waking them up, causing them fear and emotional anguish. How sad!

I cry when I remember their sweet little faces and their expressions of love for their mommy. All they wanted out of life was to not only having someone say they love them, but to spend quality time with them. Of course, that is what everyone wants. No, I was too selfish!

Yes, I know I cannot turn back the clock, but God has shown me that it is better late than never to make a U-Turn. I have asked their forgiveness and God's forgiveness as well.

He entrusted me with their precious lives and while I may not have been a Godly example then, I am presently living my life trying to be more like Jesus. I am not perfect, but I am willing and finally have learned to forgive myself.

If you are living a life of sin like I was, remember God allows U-Turns. If you are carrying guilt, give it to the Lord and remember you cannot live in the past. God can and does restore relationships. He will heal your broken heart and your family as well. It does take time, so be patient and wait on God and He will heal the hurt.

You Have Influence

When the kids were three, five, six and seven, a young pastor knocked on our door and asked if he could pick up my kids on Sunday morning for church. At that time I had no family members or not even one friend who was born again. I guess you could say I was agnostic, but I thought this would be great for the wrong reason. I always went to the bar on Saturday nights and would have a terrible hangover on Sunday. So, I figured that after I got them on the bus I could go back to sleep. Even though my motive was selfish, this event would be the start in turning the table on the devil. Total victory did not come right away, but through the years of seed planting and watering, a harvest of souls would follow. Thank you Pastor!

Sunday school teachers and bus drivers, youth workers of all ages are important! Your influence can make a difference! My four children were the first to be saved in our family. More people would follow through the years. God heard these precious intercessory prayers of my children as they interceded for their family to be saved as well. Of course with no godly life style at home as an example of a true Christian, their choices would also be influenced by the evil one. Once we know the truth as parents, you will be required you to take a stand for Christ and live the life of a dedicated Christian before your kids. They need an example and although maybe you haven't been a good example, it is not too late to make a U-Turn.

Years later when I got saved, I reminded my children that my salvation along with the salvation of their grandparents was the results of their intercessory prayers. His timing is different than ours, but nonetheless it happened. Today, I am praying for those who have strayed from God to return and serve the Lord wholeheartedly. I have already witnessed some wonderful things happening in their lives and I believe that God has great miracles planned for their lives. (Acts 16:31) God has promised that if we would believe, our whole household would be saved.

Discontent, Unthankful

When the kids were young, Ruth, Dorothy and I did housecleaning jobs. We made our own hours and the pay was good. When I got home I was so wore out that I didn't feel like cleaning my own. Although I had a new home and new furniture, I grew discontent as I compared it to the fancy homes I cleaned. I should have had a thankful heart and remembered where I had been prior to meeting Roy. Instead, I always wanted more and more things so that I could keep up with the neighbors. As I watched the daily soap operas, I grew discontent and restless for excitement. I was not happy being tied down. Discontent is a home wrecker!

I began bowling on a daytime women's league. I had a lot of fun with my two friends Lily and Teresa. Teresa and I probably were the only ones who drank during those early morning hours. I was foul mouthed and told dirty jokes. A few years later Lily became Born Again and would end up being instrumental in my spiritual birth.

When Lily got saved she quit bowling but would stop by once in a while to witness to me. I would sit there with my shot and beer listening politely. I remember laughing and saying, "Yeah, maybe one of these days when I get old, God might use me in the lives of prostitute's and strippers." I had prophesied to myself and had no idea of what I had just said.

Keep Witnessing & Interceding!

As time would pass Lily gave herself to deep intercessory prayer for me. God would bring me to her mind and she would weep and cry for my soul. Every now and then she would invite me to church. God was using not only my mom and step-dad to pray for me, but He was rising up an army of prayer warriors. They were bombarding heaven on my behalf for the spiritual battle that was going on for my soul. Never give up and stop praying for your lost family and friends. You could be only hours away from seeing them turn to God and become a flaming torch for the kingdom of God.

About this time I also met my best friend Katy, her husband Will, and their four children who were about my children's age. Katy and I had something in common, we both loved pool plus she had a pool table in her basement. Oh boy! She was the only woman I had ever met at the time who was better than me. Not only better, but also she became the top woman shooter in our county.

We joined a women's pool league that shot once a week. Three games each, with four women on a team. Of course we shot in bars that sponsored these four women teams. We would travel to a different bar each week, challenging each other. Score was kept, 2 points for winning and 1 point for every ball left on the table. At the end of the season you could win money and trophies and I loved that.

I would get drunk, then not go home when it was over, which was around ten o'clock. I never got enough, I wanted to keep drinking and shooting pool. Katy would go home to her husband and kids, but not me. This crazy driving force inside of me kept me out until the bars closed.

One Sin Leads to Another

Obviously, this took a heavy toll on my marriage. My poor husband was getting sick of this and eventually these destructive choices led to adultery. I would end up as drunk as a helpless child not able to walk or drive. In these instances I would find myself spending the night with perfect strangers picked up from the bars who never failed to take advantage of me.

Spirits of Seduction
By: Kandi Rose

At that point of drinking I was mentally and physically unable to choose right from wrong. Alcohol will impair you so bad that you will do things you thought you would never do. It is best to not to take that first drink or drugs. It will take you farther than you want to go, and keep you longer than you want to stay.

When that first encounter of adultery happened I felt so much shame and guilt. I also remember praying God, do not let me be pregnant or have a disease. It is a miracle I did not. Before we give our lives to God we ask Him for help only with big problems, those prayers are called foxhole prayers.

I could not tell anyone about this, especially my husband. Dark secrets will eat you up inside. That is one of the benefits of being saved. You can dump all your dirty laundry out to God and He cleans you up and forgives you. Repentance is a must. Repentance is turning from your actions and making a commitment to not doing it again. God knows if you are truly serious; God knows and you can't fool Him. The wonderful thing is He will give you the power to overcome any addiction.

Trying to rationalize my behavior I blamed everything and everybody. It was a pity party with a poor me mentality. If you play with fire you will get burnt. Some bad consequences happened during some of these evenings. I was robbed once, raped again, got into fights with women, almost went to jail with five driving tickets in one night, wet my pants, had diarrhea, and vomiting. Alcoholism is not a pretty sight and will strip the glamour, fun and excitement out of your life. Commercials make it look like everyone is having so much fun, yet in reality you cannot even remember if you had a good time at the end of the evening. Taking that first drink may have you off to the races, but coming in last. Do not go there! Eventually, I tuned out my conscience and the voice of God and it would ultimately wreck my home!

Roy and I would fight like crazy and even separated for a while. Then I would mellow out and not drink for weeks or even months. This made me think that I did not really have an alcohol problem.

For a little while it appeared my life was normal. I got my G.E.D. diploma just by going to the college three days taking the tests. I never took G.E.D. preparation classes and had been out of school twelve years. I was very proud of my efforts and then went to real estate school. Roy went with me to Springfield, Illinois to take the test and I received my license and began to sell real estate, which I loved. It was so rewarding helping people find their dream home. I also felt respectable. It gave me self-esteem and self-confidence.

Choices have Consequences

After a year and a half of drinking and suffering from hangovers the next morning, I finally lost my job. I never pursued this career again until a few years later, and then only for a short time.

However, I did learn about advertising, promotion, time management, sales and other business skills by going to real estate seminars. These training skills would be used years later by the devil to promote a very evil business. I opened, "Kandi Rose Productions," a Strip-O-Gram business that also became a theatrical booking agency. Later these same skills would promote the good news of Jesus Christ, through books, radio programs and Kandi Rose Ministries. God is good!

Pornography an Obsession

During my marriage with Roy a spirit of lust developed into an obsession for pornography. I started out reading bedtime romance novels. Novels with just tidbits of fornication and adultery threaded throughout the books. I would rate them as PG-13. Then I changed to books that had strong sexual language in them. I would rate them as R-Rated, but then I graduated to books that were graphic not only with language but very detailed and explicit. I'd rate them as X-Rated.

I began feeding this appetite of lust, not only with books but also with movies. So I bought X-Rated raw pornography and of course hid them from my husband and children. Later I would visit adult bookstores and watch the peep shows. Later I added an adult X-Rated movie channel to my cable TV package. If computers had been popular then, I'm positive that I would have been hooked to Internet porn. Praise God, I'm free today by the blood of Jesus!

My advice to anyone is, don't even watch underwear commercials on television; keep surfing the channels. Your mind is like a computer with a memory system. Scenes will stay in your mind, sometimes for years. Of course when you get saved, God can cleanse your mind by reading His Word. He can renew and transform your mind. (Romans 12) Constantly guard your eyes, ears, and mind. There are powerful seducing spirits that cannot be stopped by your own will power. There is Good News however, when Jesus died on the cross He said, "It is finished." He broke the power of Satan's influence to sin over us. When you accept Him and make a wholehearted commitment to live for Him, you can be set free. The chains of sin and carnal habits of every description regardless of how big or small can and will be broken by making Jesus your personal Savior.

Of course a few years later I not only viewed pornography but I became live pornography. As a Christian now, I think how sad! I used to be so proud and boastful and now the only reason I tell this story is for the purpose of assisting others in being set free. I boast now in God, and give Him the credit. I did not change myself. I could not. I tried many times to quit several habits but it would only be so long before I would be right back and even worse than before.

Freedom with no Authority Brings Slavery!

When you have freedom to do whatever you want, with no authority from God or any other human, it will lead you to destruction. Children, teenagers, married people, and even church people who desire to make their own decisions with no accountability are headed for trouble. People do not like to be accountable for their actions. "Do not tell me what to do; I will do what I want." Some say they are Christians, but do not wish to give up certain things, even though they know it is wrong. No one likes correction, even from God. When there is no accountability, it is a breeding ground for rebellion. That type of "freedom" leads to the slavery of sin.

I thought when I got divorced it would be great not answering to anybody. How sad! I am glad now to be accountable to God.

My life was getting out of control. During one of our reconciliation times, Roy and I sold our house in the suburbs of Chicago and moved to Indiana. This was three hours away and

Spirits of Seduction
By: Kandi Rose

way out in the boonies. We bought a three-bedroom home in a tiny subdivision that was in the middle of nowhere. The closest small town was about a half hour's drive. When the snow came it was piled sky high. We were only there about a year. I felt so isolated and Roy worked twelve hours or more a day. We thought if I got away from the environment of bars and other bad people, our marriage would work.

I learned that you cannot run from self. The spiritual battle for your soul goes with you. Even though evil is present, I'm so glad the Lord goes with us. He and His Angels have been with us all our lives but I was never aware of His presence. I pray that Jesus will give you a new and victorious life and keep your home and marriage from destruction. He will enable you to resist the evil and seducing spirits. You'll be able to say "no" to sin and help you make "Godly" choices.

As I had not yet allowed Jesus to become my savior at that time, worse evil followed. Since the kids had been going to church in Illinois I noticed a little church not far from our house in Indiana. So one Sunday morning we all went, which was a first for us as a family. When the altar call was given, Roy and I ran to the front and we repeated the sinner's prayer. I wanted to get rid of the guilt of adultery and make our marriage work. After the service the Pastor asked if we wanted to be baptized as a family and become members. So we were, not really understanding what we were doing, even though he tried explaining beforehand.

As I look back now after having a meaningful and real born again experience, I asked God why I was not truly born again then. He told me my motives had not been right then and I had not made a whole heart commitment to follow Him. He had knocked on my heart but I had never swung open the door. The

Bible says there is a difference of being sad about what you did, and the kind of Godly sorrow that leads to repentance.

God knows your thoughts and motives and knows if you really want to know Him. So The Holy Spirit could not come in against my will, therefore no change occurred. Since the power of God did not indwell me, I became even worse.

True Conversion brings Change

Many people in church go through the motions but there is no life changing power from God like being truly born again. When The Holy Spirit actually comes into you, there is a difference! Old things of life pass away, and all things become new. (2 Cor 5:17) You not only want to rid your life of sin so you can act differently, you also think differently. You see the evil for what it is and you do not want to be around it, much less do it. When you truly have a personal encounter with the living Jesus, you only want to please Him. His love, forgiveness, and mercy give you such a gratitude for being rescued from your sins.

Since I did not have a real born again experience, I quit church. It was the worst thing I could have done. I never gave God a chance. "Faith comes by hearing, and hearing by the word of God." Therefore, if you have not been Born Again, keep going back. Everybody needs church because it feeds the spirit of man through your worship, the preaching and prayers. You are in a great place to learn about the greatness of God and how to trust Him and trust your life to Him.

Since I made no actual commitment, which is what I really needed, I became worse and worse. My cursing became more intense and although I tried to lay the cigarettes down, I found myself smoking more, even up to two packs a day.

Seducing Spirit of Adultery

Roy worked long hours at the power plant making good money. I became bored and lonely. I was about twenty-eight years old and really did not appreciate his hard work and all the nice things he provided for us. I was selfish and thought only about myself. I was looking for something to fill the void in my life and didn't understand that peace and contentment comes from a personal relationship with Jesus.

I ended up meeting an older woman who had an eighteen-year-old son. They would come over to my house and we'd play cards while Roy was at work. I have such pain in relating these kinds of things that I did. It is shameful, but I am more interested in helping a lost world find Jesus than protecting my good name. Hopefully through this story someone else may be spared grief to themselves and others.

I hate to say it but eventfully I slept with this young guy. I felt so guilty I couldn't look Roy in the eye when he came home from work. So one day soon after, I packed all our clothes, took the four kids, this eighteen-year-old boy and headed for Illinois. How crazy! This guy didn't even work and I left a good man who loved me all because I couldn't be content. My ego was puffed up because someone showed me a little attention and desired me. (Proverbs 5-7) This scripture instructs us to beware of such behavior. If someone other than our spouse is paying too much attention to us at work, home, or even at church, be aware.

The devil makes this all seem so harmless. The casual talk or "innocent" joking leads to a relationship that can lead you

Spirits of Seduction
By: Kandi Rose

down a path of heartache and despair. It usually starts out by being friendly, then some small talk and soon a spirit of discontent for your life overcomes you. Many people end up with broken hearts, including your children from such distraction.

That relationship didn't last long. Within a short time I sent him packing back to his mama. Eventually Roy sold the house and came back to Illinois. I could not believe it, but he took me back once more. That is just like our God. Although we fail Him, he waits for us to return.

CHAPTER 6
Divorced and Desperate

Although Roy was forgiving, adultery is a hurtful thing. He never trusted me after that and always accused me of cheating whether I was or not, which caused us to constantly fight over the least things. I watched as bitterness overtook this once loving man. Of course I understand I was the one who brought a great deal of misery into his life. He's married to a good woman now but I am truly sorry for making his life so miserable. What goes around comes around and I ended up later in a relationship that would tear my heart out. The Bible says you reap what you sow and later, I would experience great heartache.

We cannot turn back the clock but we can ask God to restore all the people we have hurt in our past. We can make amends and we also have to forgive ourselves as God has. (Romans 8:1) "There is now no condemnation to those that are in Christ Jesus."

By this time all six of us were experiencing some terrible things in our lives. With a home filled with bitterness and fighting our innocent children were caught in the middle. They loved us both so much and hated to see us always wounding each other verbally as well as physically fighting. Even though I started most of the conflict, they feared for my safety. Eventually I feared for my life as both of us began to spiral out of control in the worst of ways. We were actually to the point of someone getting hurt or killed.

The kids and I finally went to my mom and step dad, who had recently been saved and ask for help. They were my refuge of safety and sanity many times throughout the years, always loving me, never giving up on me, no matter how I acted or lived. They showed me God's unconditional love. They loved me when I was unlovable just like God does. That is who Jesus died for, unlovable sinners. We all have sinned in some form or another because we were born with a sinful nature and all of us need Jesus!

Divorce is Similar to Death

Filing for divorce, was a sad time in my life. Deep down I really loved Roy and felt like I was destroying part of myself, which I was actually. Divorce is as bad as death if not worse. Whenever you see them the hurt is opened up again.

You have so many broken dreams, disappointments and loneliness. When two become one and you divorce, it's like losing a part of your body. Something's missing. The devil laughs everyday as courtrooms are filled with lives he has destroyed. He is a home wrecker!

Yes, people have a free will to choose but seducing spirits are the influence behind the scenes. That's why if the world really knew this and they would choose to live for God, life would be so different and happy. John 10:10 "The enemy has come to steal, kill, and destroy but that Jesus has come to give us life and life more abundantly."

If you have had a divorce, don't live in guilt. God knows what you have been through and He will give you the grace to get over the past. What is important is that you determine now to live for Him in the future. Let Him be your comforter and heal your broken heart. Do not live in the past. Jeremiah 29:11 "I know my thoughts for you are good and not evil to give you a good future."

Children Suffered the Most

These wrong choices had brought about many problems, but something bad was about to happen. It was about to be payday from all of these wrong choices I had made and it would affect all of us. I am saddened as I recall what happened in my children's lives. They suffered severely and emotionally. Their young years are gone now and I was not there for them. My eyes are full of tears as I write this paragraph. These were four precious children ages nine, eleven, twelve and thirteen. God had placed them in my womb for me to care for and yet they would spend their life being shuffled around from place to place.

Although I knew in my heart that I loved these children, I led a very selfish life. I failed to raise them as God had intended. God's perfect plan is for us to give our love and devotion to Him, and then train our children to love the Lord our God.

We are to not only say we love the Lord but we are to live a consistent Christian lifestyle as an example for our children. I would not be able to do this until they were teenagers. So they went through many lonely times without their mother. I'm sorry Patti, Bobby, Peggy and Dee. I have told you before and I'm publicly telling you again, thank you for forgiving me. You are such a joy in my life, as well as all my precious grandchildren and great grandchildren.

We were a fragmented family and were soon to become even more fragmented. After the divorce the four children stayed with me for a while. Roy paid child support and the bills were paid for a while. Then he fell off a ladder at work and was temporarily on disability.

The good life was about to come crashing down around our feet. We were renting a nice three-bedroom home with a fireplace and nice yard in a good neighborhood. All too soon the wonderful life Roy had provided suddenly began to crumble. He had been a great provider and a good husband, sadly enough I never appreciated what I had. The grass truly looks greener on the other side.

I soon found myself back to square one, the same place I had crawled out of when Roy and I met and married. Without Roy I once again found myself broke, lonely, and living below standards I had come to know and enjoy.

This was not only a difficult and emotionally draining time for me, but also became an emotional roller coaster for my precious children. They would be split up and bounced back and forth between Roy, my parents, and myself. Eventually, the kids would be separated from me for long periods of time.

Time slipped by

My intentions were to quickly round them as soon as I could become financially stable and we would all be together again. I never set out to give them up, but what happened to us can happen to anybody. Days turned into weeks, then months, until suddenly years had passed and their young years were gone

Spirits of Seduction
By: Kandi Rose

I had sacrificed them to search for the American dream life. Seducing spirits kept me in deception and eventually destroyed all of our lives.

I was searching for love in all the wrong places and faces. Everyone pursues happiness only to find that without God to fill that empty void in our life, we're on a dead-end street. We are like rebellious teenagers with no one to be accountable to. Life started spinning out of control and at this point I couldn't regain control.

Full of self-pity, bitterness and a hard heart, I found myself blaming others for my problems. These were severe character flaws that had been at work in me since my teen years. Now at thirty-one years of age, a mother of four and suddenly broke, I found myself unable to pay my bills.

My first instinct was to hit the bars every night of the week and drink myself into oblivion. I tended bars and worked as a cocktail waitress for a short period of time, doing anything I could to make money. I was sleeping with more men than I can remember.

One of my worst fears was being lonely with no arms around me. Roy had been affectionate until the end when our bitter fighting drove us apart. I missed that. So often a person does not appreciate the good things in life until they are gone.

Looking for Love Again

Perhaps I thought that I could replace Roy's tenderness with any willing arms. I quickly found out that if there is no love or commitment, those arms around you mean nothing. I was so empty.

In the beginning, I did not necessarily crave sex; I just wanted affectionate arms around me. In time, I started looking for sexual pleasure and soon realized this too became an addiction. A spirit of lust had come over me. I was using others and others were using me. The devil laughs at our weakness when we are caught in his terrible web. It is a miracle I didn't get a disease.

Free from Hate

During this time, Roy was so kind to give me gas money so I could travel to Tennessee to see my daddy. I had not seen him for 15 years. That is how long I carried the hate inside me. I know now only God could have lifted this from me even though I was not saved at the time. I took all of my kids to Tennessee with me.

He did not know he had four grandchildren and of course he had never seen them. After visiting him in his tiny run down house, we took a ride to Missouri to see relatives. On the way I brought up the past. I said, "Daddy I forgive you for what you did to me as a little child growing up." He became so furious at my comment that he began to curse and deny it. He even tried to jump out of the car while I was driving. I calmed him down and to this day I know God was in that car giving me the grace not to lose my usually nasty temper and react like I normally would.

God has a plan for everyone and He preserves even the unsaved people so they may fulfill their destiny. If He had not preserved me I would not be alive today much less a Christian.

Spirits of Seduction
By: Kandi Rose

Of course I was hurt tremendously that he did not or would not acknowledge his wrongful acts. I am sure that is how God must feel when we fail to acknowledge our sin against Him.

Upon seeing my dad I realized that the horrible hatred was completely gone and all I felt was pity. He was a miserable, lonely, old man with no children, grandchildren, wife or parents in his life. That is all I saw, a pitiful old man. I was free!

God did for me what I could not do for myself. I did not recognize it at the time, but the Lord graciously helped me through that ordeal. Thank God for delivering me from the hate and bitterness that had eaten away in my guts for years. If you are feeling that way toward anyone, let it go and let God help you to forgive ! What a relief not to carry that anymore!

Hope Daddy's in Heaven

Four years later daddy would die. I took two of my children with me and his only grandson., that he had never seen. By this time I was a Christian and not only did I attend daddy's funeral, I was invited to speak and was able to give my testimony. There are no surprises with God and I am so glad that He had taken the hatred from my heart.

Of course, I did not want to bring up the incest and I sure could not share anything good about daddy, so I simply talked about my heavenly daddy. My aunt was screaming at the top of her lungs uncontrollably, "he's in hell, he's in hell." She had been to the hospital to witness to him many times, and even talked to him a half- hour before he died.

Spirits of Seduction
By: Kandi Rose

The doctor said after she left he died of a heart attack while in the restroom. In the first chapter of this book I wrote that my first memory of daddy was of him messing with me while I was on the potty chair. Just remembering these terrible atrocities bring tears to my eyes. I truly hope daddy asked Jesus into his heart before he died. I want to see him in heaven.

I was no better than my daddy as far as sin goes. The same devil that enticed me, with seducing spirits, is the same devil that destroyed his life. Sin is sin. Everybody hates child molesters and it is a terrible evil but Jesus loves them and died for them as well. He died for the whole world (John 3:16).

After becoming saved I was made aware that the Holy Spirit was my counselor. One day I asked the Lord, "Why did you allow my daddy to become incestuous with me when I was such an innocent child?" I heard a small, still voice in my mind remind me that everyone has a free will and that God cannot force his will upon anyone.

Exposing Seducing Spirits

I began thinking about my free will that I had used to hurt so many people. Both, my father and I had allowed Satan to use us in bringing devastation to not only our lives but to so many others as well. We did not have the Holy Spirit to give us the power to overcome the spirits of seduction.

Jesus died to give us the power and authority over evil spirits. That's why I am using this testimony to expose the devil. When people become aware of the terrible conflict that Satan puts us through by these seducing spirits, they will hopefully come to understand why they act and think the way they do.

Spirits of Seduction
By: Kandi Rose

Only when you know where to turn for help will your life change. Only when you know the truth about Jesus and the power of His blood can you truly be set free. The choice is up to you. All you must do is choose God with your whole heart and the power of the Holy Spirit will enable you to keep that choice. You too can be, Freed by Truth! Jesus Christ!

No excuses, no blaming

No excuse will suffice when you stand before the heavenly Father to give an account of your life. The one who loves you and died for you is waiting at this very moment to set you free that you might live victoriously. You will not be allowed to blame your circumstances on others by saying, "The devil made me do it through seducing spirits."

The sacrifice has been made and one day you will be able to see the nailed scared hands of Jesus and fully understand why his blood was powerfully sufficient for you. There is no temporary pleasure or sin worth losing your soul over. Do not let a life of sin cost you any more valuable time without the Savior. Jesus has a great purpose and plan for your life. He has a better life waiting and all you have to do is choose Jesus and he will give you life.

During those months of heavy drinking my life had really bottomed out. I would drink for two days straight without eating or sleeping. Gambling on the pool table was always a driving force. I could not keep appointments.

My life was caught in a great vacuum and I was not able to make rational decisions. I was constantly missing family outings and making promises to my children I could not keep.

Days swept by because time meant nothing to me when I was in an alcoholic stupor.

I had been dating a guy who had lived a life just like I was living. He called from a government run alcohol and drug treatment center one day and told me he was in detox. He went on to say that they took women if I wanted to sign myself in. At first I thought, "I am not an alcoholic, no way." I felt my real problem was loneliness, divorce, bills, stress and all the rest.

Me, an alcoholic? No Way!

I did not picture myself as the stereotypical alcoholic lying on the street. I thought this would all pass once I found my dream life. I did not stop to think that I had already possessed, what I thought was the good life but had thrown it away because of alcohol.

That is the definition of insanity, doing the same thing over, but expecting different results. I told him that I did not need the help. After a few days with more bad experiences, I called the nurse and asked if I could join the program. I stayed in the program for five days, turning down the additional fourteen days they had offered for more treatment.

They gave me a book with some spiritual steps that could have helped. I agreed with step one, my life was unmanageable and that I was powerless over alcohol. I even admitted I was an alcoholic. I was not so sure about step two as it involved talking to God. I was not sure if there was a God. So they told me to read the agnostic chapter. The Bible says the devil has blinded our eyes from seeing the truth. I couldn't come to grips with truth at that moment.

Spirits of Seduction
By: Kandi Rose

Hind sight is 20/20. Looking back I now see that if I had believed that truth it would have made me accountable for all my other sinful actions. I really was not ready for step three, which was to make a decision to turn my life and my will over to the care of God. I did not mind turning over the alcohol problem, but I did not want to turn over my sex life, gambling, pornography, cursing and every other evil I enjoyed. I would not accept this until a few more wasted years.

Without completing steps 2 & 3, I was right back out on the street allowing Satan to use and abuse me. My poor children and family continued to suffer. Alcoholism and Drug Addiction has a ripple affect where everyone suffers. Our lives do influence others, either for good or evil

Same Ole, Same Ole

I do not think even a year went by before I called and asked if I could to go back to the program. I was confused and looking for answers. I wanted desperately to straighten my life out. I guess I thought they could fix it but I know now, they are only a source to point others to the existence of a God, who can help us. I was hurting from past failures in relationships and felt I had no hope for a good future.

Feeling worthless, I hated myself and everyone I thought had abused me. I lost my self-respect and wondered about my identity. I had no goals and felt very lonely. I felt safe locked up there and now I understand why people in jail have those same feelings. Since the environment is secure, I felt safe from my own self- destructiveness.

Spirits of Seduction
By: Kandi Rose

I was afraid that when I left the program I would start back towards the same lifestyle. My loneliness, stress and anger were enemies that could drag me back down. I needed a change. No change would come at that time. I now know why, I was not willing to surrender all to Jesus.

God is looking for people who will dedicate their whole heart and life to Him. Would you want to be married to someone who only said they loved you with their lips and their heart was far from you? Most of us have been in relationships that our partner or we tried doing what we pleased and it didn't work. God is a jealous God, (the first commandment) and He doesn't want us to put anything or anybody above Him.

Most of us will not let go of our old lifestyle. We are afraid that we will not have any fun and life will be boring. Wrong misconception, you have no idea of what excitement awaits by living the Christian lifestyle. Once you surrender your life to Him you will wonder why you waited so long. Not only will you forget the frivolous lifestyle, you'll learn the new definition of fun. Plus you will not miss any of that garbage of sin. Those past feelings will vanish when you finally surrender all to Christ.

Desperation Brought Devastation

I was divorced and desperate. Desperate is a good word to describe how I felt at that time in my life. Bills piled up and I had moved in with my mom and step-dad. Thank God for those precious and Godly people who showed me God's unconditional love. The kids were split between us, our home by now was totally wrecked. I desperately needed money to get us our own place where we could all live together again.

Spirits of Seduction
By: Kandi Rose

I searched the want ads for a job. Since real estate is based on commission, that was not my answer. I needed a steady income with reliable money. My GED was not any help and with no other training and job skills I was becoming more desperate. In Illinois, rent and utilities are not cheap. As a single mom, I just did not see how I was going to survive.

My eyes fell upon an advertisement for an Exotic Dancer in a nightclub. I thought I would go check this out since this was a job I definitely had experience in. I was 31 yrs. old at this time. I was impressed at first with this huge club with its big stage and elaborate satin curtains. They showed me the dressing rooms upstairs and it all appeared glamorous. When we talked about the pay I readily accepted. I was ignorant in what I was getting myself into.

Complete Nudity

Before I left the club the manager told me this type of dancing would be slightly different than the type of dancing I had done previously. This was full strip, complete nudity for the last few minutes of the performance. He also told me I would not only get a nightly rate of pay but would get commission on bottles of grape juice which they called champagne.

I knew how to hustle drinks, but this would be more degrading. He showed me the darkened back room where you would sit with customers who would spend big money on bottles of so called champagne. It was terrible. I hated being used like that but eventually I learned to play the game by hardening my heart. I developed an attitude that enabled me to take them for every penny in their pocket and use their credit cards to the limit. They did not care about me and I would look at them the same way. This was survival and I would survive by getting all the money I could get. I hated to go to work every night.

I acquired more sugar daddies. (Prostitution without a pimp) These men I would meet during the daytime. We'd go to fancy hotels, drink champagne and I would take their money in exchange for sex.

I started smoking marijuana with intensity. I had fallen off stage once when I was drunk and almost lost my job. So I substituted my main drug of choice, even though I still drank.

My second choice of beverage was mixed drinks because I rationalized that beer and shots were my downfall. I felt I needed something to dull my mind and desensitize me. I needed that temporary peace to deal with this life of seduction.

The other dancers were fuzz brained as well. This was a job nobody either wanted or could do with a clear head. Each of the girls had their own type of drug or alcohol they used to be able to cope with this lifestyle.

The money is the draw and keeps women imprisoned in this jail without bars. Some who read this may have no pity for strippers or prostitutes. I certainly do because I was one. You never know what brought these girls into this situation. I now know that the devil is the influence through seducing spirits.

Jesus Offers Forgiveness

Jesus loves all people who are caught up in all types of sin. When lost people get a revelation of their sins and learn the truth, Jesus is there to forgive them. When they turn from their ways of sin with repentance, they will experience a life of righteousness and never be the same. They will be forgiven from their old lifestyle and will be given a new lifestyle. I am proof it is possible.

I was awakened one Sunday morning with my mom and step dad asking me to go with them to church. I was living with them at the time and may have agreed because of feeling obligated ... nonetheless, I accepted.

During worship I started sobbing. I had to walk out to the car. I sat there and cried my eyes out. I remember thinking I wish I could be like all those wonderful people. I reasoned however, that I could not and I needed that big money to put my family back together.

God's Voice Calling, I ignored

Of course, now I know that the devil was lying and it was the Holy Spirit calling me and that was why I was so broken and crying.

I now realize that all those good people had been sinners at one time before God changed them. They may not have been at the depths of sin as I had, but sin is sin with God. They were only good now because they had taken on the righteousness of God through the blood of Jesus. I know now that not all people who sit in the church are saved. There are many who have sin in their life and God is dealing with them much like He dealt with me. Being a church member does not save you and it takes the power of the Holy Spirit to live a consistent Godly lifestyle. Years later I would backslide and experience a terrible spiritual battle for my soul. I now have compassion for others stuck in that spiritual rut.

I continued to dance in the nightclub. It sickened me however and it really brought my self-esteem to an all time low causing me to eventually quit. About a week later that club was busted and had I been there I would have gone to jail. I now had a steady boyfriend who was about ten years younger than me. One of his friends was about to get married and asked me if I would dance at his bachelor party. He said that he would pay me generously for a half hour. I said I would, telling him my boyfriend would be my bodyguard and there would be no touching.

Off we went that night with my big boom box, elaborate costumes and props. I made lots of tips along with the base pay. I gave my boyfriend a small portion and I kept the rest. I was excited and to me this was great. I got to do what I loved to do, which was to dance. Best of all there was no grubby paws touching me. I viewed this as entertainment now and felt self-worth.

X-Rated Business

That evening was a huge turning point in my life. This destructive choice would set me on a course of an evil but successful X-Rated Lifestyle. I always had a mind for business that developed through my short real estate career. I had been good at school and would soon put that knowledge to work for the devil. God gives us talents and abilities that He desires for us to use to further His Kingdom. Unfortunately, many of us use these to further the work of Satan. I would be used and use others to an even greater extent.

Spirits of Seduction
By: Kandi Rose

After dancing that evening for my boyfriend's friend, I was greatly inspired by Satan to get business cards and start doing this kind of entertaining for private parties. In a short period of time it became very profitable and I soon discovered the non- Christian society viewed this as good entertainment.

I called my business, "Kandi Rose Productions." I felt that I was actually producing good clean fun. I thought it was clean because there was no touching or prostitution involved. How ridiculous! Soon, women were asking for male strippers for their bachelorette and birthday parties. So I advertised and held auditions for male strippers. When I went out to regular public nightclubs for a social night out, I would scout for men and women I could hire.

Used by the devil

Not only was Satan using me, I was finding others that would fall prey to this kind of a lifestyle. Let's face it my friends, you are going to become an evil influence or a Godly influence in this world. I am now letting God use me for His righteous cause. The devil will not be using me anymore!

Theatrical Booking Agency

I used to think this was glamorous and so exciting. I was not only looked up to as a celebrity and an entertainer, but now I was considered a talent scout, a booking agent. In a short time I had twenty-six people working for me. The business snowballed from just male and female private strip shows into a Theatrical Booking Agency. I booked men and women into nightclubs where we all performed a two-hour choreographed show that consisted of all types of entertainment.

Spirits of Seduction
By: Kandi Rose

I provided magicians; break dancers, hypnotists, and of course scantily clad dancers, performing skit scenes. I had two men who could dance on roller skates. I had one dress as a clown and named him Rose-O after me, to dance on roller skates during intermission. I also got into the act as a vampire coming out of a coffin. For the grand finale I did a swan dive into two of my male dancer's arms from a high point off stage. I started looking for higher points to jump from. That dare devil spirit probably would have brought physical harm or even death. It is hard to believe that I really did those things. I am so changed now. I advertised this business to the hilt. I put ads in the newspapers, yellow pages, magazines, on radio stations, and even a Billboard across the street from a Drive-In Movie.

Putting on the Ritz

I had a commercial on Cable Television. In the commercial I had a limo drive my dancers and myself to the front door of a nightclub. Upon arriving in the limo, the commercial started with the camera focusing in on the leg of one of my female dancers as the back door opened. Then we all proceeded to exit the limo arm in arm onto a carpeted runway.

We were all dressed in tuxedos and formal wear. Then the commercial showed the dancers and myself in costume, individually dancing. The television station came and shot this on location. This particular commercial was aired about 40 times a day.

My commercial appeared on MTV, Nashville Network, ESPN and news networks as well as several other stations. I also danced on the Lake County Fairgrounds Stage and had a promotional table set up to advertise the business. I joined the

Round Lake Chamber of Commerce and had a promo table set up at The Business and Home Expo.

I was Ms. AutoFest at the Arlington Park Race Track for their huge Car Show. About 40,000 people came and I was dressed in a long black evening gown with a white satin banner that read, "Ms. AutoFest." I awarded about 200 trophies to the winners of the car show. A male and female dancer was continually by my side along with Katy, my manager. I had professional pictures of each of us and we autographed them at my promo table.

I also was deemed, Lake County's most "Prominent Showgirl" during the Lake County Auto Show, held at the County Fairgrounds. I walked around in a bikini, with a parasol having my picture taken alongside numerous antique and muscle cars. I awarded trophies and signed autographs.

Another similar situation was the McHenry Boat and Auto Show where there were trophies, autographs, and pictures taken again.

I was an Auction Item

A well known worldwide charitable organization that holds picnics and auctions every year for a fundraiser used me as an item to bid on. I stood in front of the auctioneer in formal wear while he held bids for one of my performances. The wives of the town's rescue squad bid 150.00 on me to perform a full strip for their husbands during the day at the rescue station.

Eventually my boyfriend and I broke up and my best friend Katy became my manager and bodyguard. She would stand with me by the door or near me with her one hand inside her coat. They would ask if she had a gun and she would just smile. She told me after I got saved that she had prayed many times when we were in some very bad situations.

Angels guarding

I now know that God had angels guarding us. Katy always acted tough and I credited our safety to my attitude of being in control and setting the crowd straight beforehand. Thank you Lord! It is true, the devil can give you boldness to do or go into some very dangerous situations. Likewise, as Christians we must allow God to use us wherever there are lost sheep to rescue.

On three different occasions we volunteered to work fundraisers for local town Chamber of Commerce's. These were golf fundraisers. We hopped on the booze golf cart, with me dressed in a bikini and parasol. Katy drove and I would stand when possible and dance. One time when driving, as she went under a tree, I ducked just in time as a tree branch almost wacked me. We laughed and laughed. I really enjoyed fundraisers and felt I was doing a good deed and was also getting good press and advertisement as well.

During the Christmas season, Katy and I went to the North Chicago VA Hospital. I dressed in a corset costume with tights (not showing skin) and danced up and down the hallways popping into rooms and handing out candy. On one occasion we went to a nursing home where one of my male dancers put on a sequined costume and danced on roller skates in and out around the seniors who were sitting at tables. I also danced in a white beaded corset costume with black tights underneath.

Giving more than Entertainment, Jesus

I will never forget what my born again friend, Lily, said to me as I bragged about this event. She said, "It was great that you wanted to make them smile and be happy but God wants you to give them something that will last forever, Jesus." I now know what she meant. Ever since I turned my life over to Christ, I no longer promote myself I promote Jesus.

Yes, I was having fun doing all this. Katy and I would cut up and joke all the while counting the money. I loved to dance and was respected and recognized in the upper class business world. Even wives and girlfriends were hiring my dancers and myself.

I even danced in the basement of one of the local town police stations. I was hired by one of the police officers for another officer's party. The wife of a wealthy funeral home owner had me come to their house for her husband's birthday party. Dressed as a vampire, I climbed into one their coffins. When the music started I opened it and came out dancing. There were so many unusual places and people that used my services.

Sin is pleasurable for a season. That means it is fun for just a short time. Afterward, however, there is such an empty feeling. At this time I was not feeling any guilt or shame. I was proud of whom I had become but I had no peace, contentment and no serenity. Something was missing and I thought it was because I did not have a steady guy or my children with me. What was missing was the true love of my life, Jesus.

I remember a few times that a particular thought would cross my mind. The thought was, "What if I do become Lake

County's richest woman because I was headed that way, and still die and go to hell?" I did not know it then there is a verse in the Bible that talks about that. (Matthew 16:26) I had never read that scripture so I know God was talking to me.

After the glamour of the day would fade, I would lay on my bed just restless and unable to sleep. I would smoke pot trying to relieve stress. I would light up almost every hour from the time I woke up until I went to bed. I did not want my buzz to fade. I had become addicted to pot instead of alcohol because I could not run my business drunk all the time.

Late hours were spent under the influence of pot, which I thought was the reason for my awesome creativity in advertising techniques. Satan gives creative abilities that can become very successful. Just look at Hollywood producing such evil content through movies, music and magazines.

Hear, see, speak & read no evil

There is an abundance of sex, violence and language that sickens both God and I. R-Rated and X-rated productions are made to lead others into temptation, seducing spirits. Beware of what you see, hear or read. Guard your mind, your spirit and your soul. God gives us the ability to choose, so choose your freedom through Christ, not slavery to lust and pornography as I once did.

I now choose to be under the inspiration of the Holy Spirit and be creative for the Lord. That is why I am writing this book. God is the creator and we are made in His image. He has given us the ability to be creative and used either for His glory or for Satan's purposes. It is our choice. I choose the Lord, how about you?

I would often be up all hours of the night because my mind would not shut down and let my body sleep. Smoking pot usually relaxed me but I found that there was no rest for the wicked. I felt such emptiness.

I found myself picking up a Bible that mom had given me and I began to read bits and pieces of the book of Psalms. This whole book was foreign to me but after reading a little, my mind would be at peace and I would be able to sleep. I knew there was something different about this book called the Bible.

I was unaware that God was slowly drawing me towards knowing Him. He knew I was lost and therefore had compassion on me. He knew me when I was in my mother's womb. (Psalm 139)

He had been there all through those years of pain and suffering. Nevertheless, He saw me as valuable, precious, and special in His eyes. I was one of the millions upon millions that He had died for. I was about to be found.

Does a spiritual realm influence our choices?

Is there an invisible, unseen Spiritual realm that influences our choices? Are there demons and a devil? Is there a God, Jesus, a Holy Spirit, and angels? Do our choices have consequences that will determine our destiny? Are there seducing spirits influencing our choices that will ultimately lead to our destiny?

Spirits of Seduction
By: Kandi Rose

I'm convinced this spiritual realm exists. As you read this chapter, I believe you will too. Review your own past choices and ponder certain occasions that you thought were just lucky, unlucky, or just coincidence. Without doubt there was an evil influence that wrecked havoc on my life. I firmly believe also that there is a God who intervened on my behalf many times through the Spiritual realm. Even in reliving this testimony I am overwhelmed by God's love and mercy.

My mom, step dad, and especially my children as well as friends and others who knew me can definitely attest to this spiritual miracle. I call it a miracle because when you have tried to change yourself as many times as I had, you have to know it is supernatural. The multiple addictions, the hard heart, the bitter spirit, none of these could have been changed by my own will power. I tried many times.

To some degree there were certain addictions, habits and attitudes I could manage to abstain. I could stay clean from these addictions for days, weeks and even months; but in the end I would succumb to those seducing spirits. Often when I did go back and pick up my old habits, the addictions were stronger than before.

CHAPTER 7
The Choice that affected my Destiny

A Spiritual battle for my soul was about to be won in the heavenlies. About a week before being saved, my mom had a horrendous nightmare. She said she could not tell if it was a dream or a vision because it was so real to her. My mother and my step-dad, Lily and countless other Christians from various churches were bombarding heaven on my behalf. It's called intercessory prayer, or standing in the gap for someone.

The Vision

One evening mom began to relate a vision/dream of me being put naked in a large wicker basket. She saw two beings trying to cram the lid down on my head. She also had a perverted vision of me, which sickened her with disgust.

Now my mother had a great ministry in intercessory prayer. Mom had suffered physically in her body all her life with different ailments, but her compassion for lost and hurting people had never wavered. Through all of her physical sufferings she kept the joy of the Lord and looked beyond herself to pray for hundreds of people. She had unconditional love and was never critical or judgmental. She realized she was a sinner once and needed Jesus just as much as I did.

Following the vision, mom said that for the first time in her life she felt totally appalled and disgusted with my evil lifestyle. So much so, she angrily got up and turned my picture around that hung in the dining room.

Spirits of Seduction
By: Kandi Rose

While up until this time mom had never given up praying for me. Now, through the natural eye it looked like the devil had finally conquered me, and the battle was forever lost. I am sure the enemy had put this discouraging thought in her mind that I would never change. Those thoughts were probably put there more times than one could count, but prayer changes people and situations.

Never stop praying for your loved ones. Remember, the darkest hour is just before the dawn ... the light is coming. God loves doing the impossible, and when He does, only He can get the credit or glory for the miracle.

I certainly was at the most evil point in my life. Although I was out of control, I certainly did not think I was. I thought all was well and that I was doing great. I proudly proclaimed that no one, not even a man could get me to quit what I was doing because that's how much I enjoyed this business. I was determined to be independent and motivated to become the richest woman in town and give my children everything they could want in life.

Spiritual Warfare

As soon as mom turned my picture around with such disgust, the Holy Spirit spoke to her. She recognized the devil's strategy. Satan was using a reverse psychology in getting her to stop praying for me. She became so mad at the devil that she immediately entered into intense spiritual warfare for me. She rebuked those seducing spirits, verbally casting them out of my life by pleading the blood of Jesus. She said, "in the name of Jesus Christ, I bind you Satan and command you to loose my child, all evil spirits have to leave now, in Jesus name!"

The main thing I can tell you, prayer works. My deliverance was set in motion through this prayer. The spiritual battle began and war was declared. The Holy Spirit and the angels were dispatched on my behalf and a week later I was saved and set free from all those tormenting and seducing spirits. A series of events was orchestrated to complete my deliverance and salvation. It was not coincidental. Nothing is coincidental.

More Intercessors

A short time prior to this taking place, two ministers from Lily's church felt compelled to go to my office parking lot to pray for my salvation. I will always be grateful for the spiritual obedience of Brother Paul and Brother Wayne.

They were confident God would save me, what they did not know was I would become a member of their tiny church, not my mother's church. They would also become two of the most important and greatest male mentors in my life. Their ministries would impact my life to help me walk the walk.

Later, people would come up to me from various churches that did not know my family or me and told me how they had prayed for my salvation. They had stretched their hands out to my huge Billboard and asked God to close my business and save the people. Wow!

Lily and I knew each other from our bowling days but had never really hung out with each other. At the time we were not close friends, but God began to give her a burden and a compassion for my soul. My mother and Lily had become good friends and why not, they had the same heavenly Father.

Invited to church

Lily continued to stop by the bowling alley and witness to me. She was very unlike me. She was not a drinker or a wild person. She was a quiet housewife who had been married as a teen to the same man all her life. Yet, she did not judge me. God gave her compassion for me as a lost sheep that needed The Good Shepherd. She did what Christians are supposed to do, pray and witness.

Lily had asked me several times to come to her church but I always made excuses and would say, "maybe one of these days I will surprise you. Then on Monday night, March 4, 1984 I suddenly found myself saying yes.

It was ironic that on that very night I was booked to do a fundraiser. A Lake County Judge was up for re-election and was having a dinner and candlelight bowl at a popular bowling alley. I had donated one of my performances in the form of a coupon as one of the prizes for the bowling winners.

X-Rated to G-Rated Date

After the dinner, during the cocktail hour, I brought a male and female dancer with me to perform a skit scene that was not a strip but a dance drama in scanty costumes. I had just started to date a recovering alcoholic who I really liked and he was my date that night.

I forgot that I had this booking when I agreed to go to church, but I am confident that God knew. After the show was over, I looked at my watch and thought I was a half hour late and almost did not go. I went anyway and if I had known I was an

Spirits of Seduction
By: Kandi Rose

hour late I would not have gone. That old saying, better late than never really applied to me that night. I told my date we were going to church and since I was driving, he had no decision in the matter.

Now I find it rather humorous to think about what an unusual date this would be for him. We started the evening X-Rated and would finish it G-Rated. I doubt very many have ever had a dating experience as weird as this was.

While driving to the church I was thinking, why are you going to church? You just came from doing a show and look at who you are? You are a stripper and owner of a stripping business. This is crazy I thought. Now I fully understand that our choices can be influenced by seducing spirits to keep us from our purpose and destiny.

Not dressed for the occasion

Lily said they were in a revival and a former gang member and drug addict from Chicago was preaching. My interest was piqued immediately. When we walked in Brother John was preaching up a storm. My date and I slipped into the back pew and I was feeling downright weird. I had a long fur coat over a slinky purple satin jumpsuit, silver high heels, and big floppy velvet hat with a purple satin choker on my neck.

Consequently, I left my coat on because I was definitely not dressed like these church folks. Matter of fact I must have stood out like a sore thumb. Although I noticed only smiling faces. We had just smoked some marijuana on the way there and still had some left in my purse.

Brother John was the evangelist and he was one very loud and excited preacher. He was so passionate for Christ. I now remember thinking about the change God had made in this man and even in my condition I saw the joy, enthusiasm and the passion he had for lost souls.

True joy was something I did not have. Yes, my business was dancing, which provided a so call joy, but this joy was different. I saw him cry and plead for people to be saved.

Feelings of Conflict

Since we were an hour late we missed a lot of the message, nevertheless the Holy Spirit began dealing with me immediately. He was urging me to surrender my life to Jesus and the evangelist came back to our pew and said, God has a miracle for you. There were other words God said to me through him that night, but this is the phrase I remember. I did not get saved that night because I quickly got up and left the church. I was very uncomfortable and uneasy.

My feelings were so conflicted that night and of course we can all guess who was providing those feelings of conflict in my spirit, the enemy of my soul. Once we got in the car, something strange happened. I found myself scanning the radio for a preaching station. I had never ever done anything like that before. I always had my radio tuned to the latest top hits as loud as I could crank it and kind of dancing in my seat as I drove. This was a real switch.

As we lit up a joint of pot we discussed the possibility that God existed. I realize now that the Lord was revealing Himself to me and I was beginning to awake spiritually. The

Bible says we can't come to Him unless the Holy Spirit draws us. This was the first of a series of incidences indicating that God was drawing me to salvation.

The next great event in my life would become the best night of my life. It was the choice that affected my destiny. I was soon to be, freed by Truth!

The revival service we attended had been on a Monday evening but we did not go back the next night. After their Tuesday night service my friend Lily, along with some of the church people, the Pastor and Evangelist went to a nearby restaurant. I had recently moved my office to Katy and Will's basement. That evening I received a devastating phone call that was more than I could bear. I thought that two of my children were going to be put into a foster home. I could handle almost anything in life but this was my rock bottom. I was hysterical and needed peace of mind to deal with this crisis.

Perfect Timing

Immediately after that alarming phone call, the phone rang again and it was Lily calling from the restaurant to see if I wanted to join them. I was crying and said no thanks. Lily told me later that she did not really want to call me but felt the Holy Spirit strongly urge her to get up and call. This was strange indeed since we never really socialized together except for bowling. For her to call for anything, much less to call this time of night was very odd.

After I hung up the phone a spiritual battle took place for my heart, mind and soul right there in my office. I was so distraught.

Spirits of Seduction
By: Kandi Rose

My heart was so hard that not much could bother me anymore. When it came to my kids however, God knew this was a sensitive area that was dear to me. Even though from all appearances it looked like I did not care because of my lifestyle. God knew my motivation was to make money so my kids and I could get back together.

Sin was keeping me longer than I wanted to stay and it was keeping me longer than I expected because time slipped away, day after day, week after week, year after year. Sin will actually keep you burdened with broken dreams and broken relationships as you continue in sin.

Who you listening to?

Remember the cartoon that shows an angel on one shoulder telling the cartoon character to make good choices? Then on the other shoulder a guy with a pitchfork telling him to make evil choices? That's the best way I can describe this invisible battle being waged for my mind, heart and soul. The Holy Spirit was telling me to give my life to Jesus so that I could know true peace and forgiveness. On the other hand seducing spirits were telling me to not be foolish and throw away my business and my chance to be rich.

It was a difficult decision because I really enjoyed my newfound career and I loved to dance. People admired and respected me and treated me as a Hollywood entertainer. Everywhere I went people recognized me from the commercials and personal appearances.

Still, there was this emptiness and a void in my life that I had attributed to not having met my dream man or been able to get my kids back. I had forgotten that I had those things at one time and let them go because I did not understand their worth and was not satisfied.

People, places and things cannot give you true serenity. We were created to have an intimate relationship with God through His Son, Jesus Christ. People say they have peace, but if there is sin in their lives, they are just being deceived by Satan. God is Holy and we must live a Godly lifestyle in order to be intimate with Him.

Since we were born with a sinful nature a sinless sacrifice, Jesus, came to die for us so we could have the power to be able to say no to sin. It's His blood that was shed on Calvary's Cross that makes us Holy.

It's our responsibility to choose and accept the Good News, and then be willing to turn from our old sinful lifestyle.

At a Crossroad

I was in a spiritual battle and the Spirit of God was calling for a decision. I called my mom's house and my oldest daughter Patti, answered the phone. She was about sixteen years old at the time and living with my mom and step dad.

I began relating to her what had just transpired and using her as a sounding board as I told her about the crossroads I had reached in my life. It was a crossroads decision and I was crying because I needed peace desperately. I felt like I was losing my mind.

Spirits of Seduction
By: Kandi Rose

At that time, I did not know what the word repentance meant but the Holy Spirit was faithfully guiding me into the truth. He said I would have to let go of my lifestyle, the same lifestyle that I had tried to shake off and could not. At this point God was building faith in me to believe that it was possible. This was the time and He was telling me to surrender everything. He told me to not worry how it would happen but to have a childlike faith to trust him.

Repent means turn away from and go in the other direction … and make a U-Turn. That is what so amazing about being saved, we do not do it, it is a miracle from God.
All we have to do is make a sincere, wholehearted commitment and really mean it, and allow Him be in control of our life. We are not just to talk it but also to walk it.

Supernatural Miracle

After a few minutes of mulling this hard decision over with my daughter, I asked her to put mom on the phone. I was crying so hard. I said, "mom, I want to give my life to Jesus," and she started crying with tears of joy as you can imagine. She said she would lead me in a prayer to confess my sins and I would be saved. (Romans 10:9-10) I do not remember the exact words but God heard and He knew that I was crying out from the depths of my sinful despair and that I really meant it.

This is the biggest, greatest miracle of all. It is a miracle that cannot be seen with the natural or the physical eye. The Holy Spirit actually comes into your life and we become the temple for God to live in and work through. It is God who gives us the power and ability to live a holy lifestyle because we now are His children. (John 1:12)

Spirits of Seduction
By: Kandi Rose

Wow! When that prayer ended a peace came over me like something I have never experienced before. My eyes are filled with tears as I recall that glorious night because I knew I belonged to God from that day forward. He was my Heavenly daddy and everything was going to be all right. Childlike faith was there. Just as a little child does not worry about tomorrow or the future, I did not either.

After we prayed I said, "mom, could you call Lily at the restaurant and see if they would open the church doors so I can go in and pray?" She said that she would call me right back and guess what? They were still there and said they would meet me at the church. I asked mom if she would go and she joyfully agreed. I went to pick her up because she did not drive.

I was so excited and full of anticipation. You would have thought I had won a million dollars. Better yet, I had just met the love of my life, Jesus. I searched my closet for something decent to put on and everything I owned was sexy, low cut, tight and revealing.

My Spiritual Eyes Opened

For the first time in my life I wanted to be modest. I found a low cut dress and safety pinned the neck. Amazingly I did not want to expose myself. That was a miracle because if you had known me before you would understand the victory in that one choice. In a moment's time my eyes were opened to righteous living and I am modest to this day. I started to recognize good and evil and no longer wanted any suggestion of evil in my life. Prior to this happening I had been smoking pot, but my mind was now clear and I no longer wanted to smoke anything anymore. I would usually light up every forty-five minutes, non-stop throughout the day.

I got in the car to go pickup my mother and as a natural response, I started to light a cigarette. At that time I was smoking two packs of cigarettes a day and had for twenty-four years. I was a certified chain smoker.

Here is another Spiritual battle. In that moment I heard the voice of the Lord say, "Come all the way." Needless to say I was getting another message of why I should not do it. I obeyed God's voice; I rolled down the window and threw the whole pack out including the lighter. After all, I would not be smoking pot or cigarettes. I haven't smoked since 1984.

I want you to know that I had such an excitement stirring within me that when I got to mom's house I was laughing and crying at the same time. Finally, after all these years I was experiencing something new, tears of joy and so was mom. It was probably around 11 pm when we entered the church and somewhere around midnight before we left.

When we entered the church I literally ran to the altar and fell down crying. I was so aware of God's Holy presence that I held my hands around the neck of that dress to make sure I was not exposed. For the first time in my life I truly felt shame and guilt for the life I had led. I had been so brazen and hard hearted but now in His Holy Presence I saw myself for who I really was.

The Search Is Over

I told God I was sorry and confessed all my sins. I cried and cried at the realization that I had wasted the life he had given me. Then peace came over me as he spoke to my heart and mind. I knew in my spirit that he loved me and I was totally forgiven. I experienced at that moment as I still do today, the fullness of joy in His Presence. There is love, forgiveness and power when you learn to trust Him. I am still amazed today at His Great Love and Mercy toward all. He truly is a good Shepherd who seeks out the lost. I am so glad He found me and I am glad I did not refuse when he called me.

When I got up from that altar the old Kandi Rose was gone. The old life was put to death and I was raised with Christ to a new life. The seductive lifestyle was buried and a lifestyle of holiness was resurrected, holy because of Jesus death on the cross. I not only found peace, but I found a personal relationship with the love of my life, Jesus.

Jesus is my closest intimate companion, who has never failed to be there for me. I never realized all those years that he loved me and had been there all along.

I know now the meaning of the Bible verse, "cast all your care upon Him". When I got up from that altar, I did not have a worry or a care because I gave it all to the Lord Jesus. What a feeling! It is hard to describe it, but to those who have met Jesus, you understand. I had no shame or guilt. He had forgiven me! I felt very loved and special to think that He would reveal Himself to me, a woman who had been a stripper, prostitute and addict.

After I read the Bible, I understand that it was people just like me that Christ had died. I was a sinner and He loved me as though I had never done anything wrong. Regardless of how big or little one may consider their sin to be, that sin cannot enter into heaven. Every one of us either needed or will need His forgiveness because that is what the cross and his shed blood are all about. I was lost but now I am found!

Got to Tell

The next day I was on the phone calling downtown Chicago telling them I was saved and to take my huge Billboard down. I remember the day it was put up. Katy and I sat in front of it amazed and excited, knowing this would make us rich. She told me later she was not doing it for riches but because of our friendship.

Seeing the billboard disgusted me now and being rich suddenly became unimportant compared to this new life I now had with Jesus. My whole mindset about my business completely changed. I saw it as evil now and wanted no part of it. I called all of my advertisers, employees, the nightclubs and dissolved any and all business with them.

I proudly proclaimed to them, I am saved now. I was so happy and carefree, even knowing there would be no more riches and the fact I was now unemployed did not matter. I was okay with being broke and poor because I knew I was in good hands. God was now in control, not me.

Jesus Made the Difference

I did not crave any of those addictions anymore either. I only craved His Presence, His Word, church and being with other Christians, praying and witnessing. It was awesome! God's Spirit in me made all the difference. He brought about the change. I only had to be willing.

Spirits of Seduction
By: Kandi Rose

Very shortly after, I moved in with mom and papa, my step dad. They were my greatest examples and mentors along with Lily. The next evening was a Wednesday and I went back to church with Lily instead of my folks. I felt that her church was where I should be since I had experienced such a wonderful meeting with Jesus previously at that altar. There is no place more special to you than the place that you get saved. It was as though I exchanged marriage vows to Jesus to love, honor and obey him.

The Bible says that we become one with Christ. In that little church there were so many loving people who accepted me and made me feel like one of their family. They did not care about what kind of woman I had been. They were excited to see the miracle that God had wrought in my life.

About a week later, Lily and I were cleaning the church, even the toilets and I was somewhat amused. Here I was, the so-called, "star of Lake County," cleaning toilets. I was both thrilled and humbled to do something for the Lord.

This church was different than mother's church. Lily's church did not believe in women wearing slacks, shorts, makeup and jewelry, so I just refrained. I wanted to please God so much it did not matter what the demands might be.

I now know that God is looking at our heart, actions, and attitudes. Of course, it is pleasing to God when we dress modestly and Christians should never do anything or wear anything that would be an obvious temptation to others. It was good for me to have righteous restrictions placed upon me after coming out of such a wild and crazy life.

God, My Provider

I was now broke, had no business and no job. That too was a good thing because I got to experience God as my provider. Nothing is coincidence or luck. God uses people to meet our needs and makes opportunities arise for employment.

My first job was a nanny, watching three children. What a switch. I made in a week what I used to make in a half hour. I was however, so contented and happy. Money was no longer an issue or priority. Six months later I was asked to manage the world's largest Salvation Army Thrift Store.

The greatest miracle other than my salvation was the fact that I did not have to put my children in a foster home. God worked it all out. Too often we try to make deals with God by saying, "God if you'll do this or that, then I'll live for you," then we go back on our word with God and don't fulfill our promises. I knew by the circumstances surrounding my conversion that there was definitely a God caring for me and that I needed to keep my vows to Him.

God is real and He is A Spirit. Even though I can't see Him, I know He is there and has been all my life. He is the one that makes good things happen in my life. I now refer to it as a "God hook-up." The bad events are a "devil hook-up."

It is so important to stay in God's Word, to pray, to be faithful to His cause and share your life and testimony with those around you. There is a Spiritual battle of seducing spirits that take place every day of our lives and we must choose if we are going to be led astray or follow God's way.

Spirit of Lust

One of the last addictions in my life to go was lust. About 2 weeks after I was saved, I heard a sermon about Samson and Delilah. (Judges 16) I had surrendered all my other addictions and sin except fornication, which is sex outside of marriage.

When I heard this sermon, I knew God was speaking to me. Here I was at another crossroads and I knew God had given me the same supernatural power as he had Samson.

I had personally experienced this for myself, not just from hearing or reading about someone else's life. I knew I did not produce this kind of power on my own.

The evil one was telling me, God does not want you to be alone and lonely. Besides, it is only one man; you are not sleeping with anyone else. What a liar. Satan will tell us anything to get us to compromise and lose our intimate relationship with the one who loves us and gave His life for us. I remember saying, God, do not take sex away from me. After all, I gave you my business, pot, alcohol, pornography, gambling, cursing, even cigarettes but please not sex. I was crying when I left church but had not surrendered during the altar call.

Visiting with Brother John the next day, I was very distraught and through tears told him the situation and how I had surrendered all to Jesus except sex. I tried rationalizing and minimizing. After hearing me, he spoke with such compassion, "I will pray for you to marry a Christian husband." I was so let down. I did not want to hear that, I wanted to hear how it was good that all the other old garbage was gone and that this would eventually be okay. The Bible clearly states, "no fornicators shall inherit the kingdom of God." (Galatians 5:19)

I was totally upset and actually felt like going out and committing suicide. That was certainly not God's voice that I was hearing. I was crying hard as I struggled spiritually with the realization that God wanted me to submit to total abstinence. I did not want to give it up, simple as that. I was not willing. I went home and told my mother. We cried together and God gave her the right words to speak to me. She could not lie and tell me what I wanted to hear. The truth is what sets us free and that truth is in God's word, the Bible.

I knew I did not want my old life back. I loved this new relationship with Jesus. I also did not want those other addictions to come back on me. I did not want to lose the power I was experiencing and knew I could become like Samson if I continued to sleep with this man. Was sex worth losing my pure relationship with Jesus? Was it worth losing my peace, and joy and missing heaven? No! After all, look what Jesus gave up to give me very life. He surrendered all, could not I?

Freed from Lust

I not only could, I would and yes I did. I made another choice that affected my destiny. I called my boyfriend and gave him my decision. He said that my decision was fine with him and that we could continue to date. I was thrilled and to celebrate we went to a bowling alley and shot pool without gambling.

He talked me into going to a motel room just to watch TV and have a private place to be together and I said okay. Bad decision on my part and it was just dumb, dumb, and dumber.

Spirits of Seduction
By: Kandi Rose

The Holy Spirit was living in me and was speaking loud and clear when I walked in that room. It did not take long and I started crying. This was a switch for me because I never had a conscience or thought I was doing wrong pertaining to any type of sexual activity. I sensed the presence of my Heavenly Father immediately in the room. The best example I can give to describe that feeling is like this: if your wonderful and loving spouse were observing and it would break their heart.

This of course went far beyond that. This was The Holy One, the Almighty God who loves us and created us for His pleasure. He was right there as he always had been during all those other times of sexual promiscuity during my life. I just did not have His Holy Spirit inside me to recognize His existence prior to this.

I felt so ashamed that I literally ran out of there. I was glad I had not done anything. When I got in the car and sped out of there it hit me. God helped me win that spiritual battle and it was monumental. Lust had been defeated by His power, not mine. I started crying again but not from sadness but joy as I realized what had just happened.

Spiritual Virgin

Victory, oh sweet victory! I felt so clean and pure. I realize now I was spiritually a virgin and God had forgiven all my sins including all the sexual sins as well. Awesome! I am still moved when I think of what a loving, caring, forgiving, and merciful God we have. You cannot tell me that seducing spirits are not at work trying to devastate our lives through our wrong choices.

What a miracle! I was able to abstain from this enticement for many years. Finally I had true self-worth and self-esteem. It does not come from a career, material things, or even human relationships. It comes from knowing you have no intentional sin in your life before a Holy God.

You can rest in the fact that you are forgiven, loved and honoring Him with your life. Pleasing God is all I want to do. You cannot please people all the time but what is important is pleasing Him.

Sin separates us from God

One example of a true Christian lifestyle is how God's plan for marriage was intended. When you are married to a good and loving spouse, you would not want to do anything bad to destroy that relationship. Sin will separate you from God and it will build a wall between you and His Holy presence. You can't have a pure relationship with Him nor can you have a pure relationship with your spouse or family when addiction puts up a wall between those relationships. You cannot straddle the fence and live any way you want. Keeping any type of intentional sin no matter how big or small ruins a pure relationship with a Holy God.

My life was definitely filled with lots of extreme sinful content. When you think your life is not as bad as mine was, remember sin is still sin. No sin will enter Heaven unless we ask for God's forgiveness.

When we allow our lifestyle to be changed by God, we will have greater peace and serenity than can ever be found in any of the old garbage you once used for happiness. It feels great to be forgiven and have a new life. No, we do not become perfect, but true Christians do not keep intentionally sinning. When we mess up we ask for God's forgiveness as quickly as possible and experience His forgiving love. (I John 1:9)

Do not continually sin on purpose. Repent means to turn away from, to no longer be involved in that sin in any way. If you would like a lifestyle change right now say this prayer out loud as you read it:

Lord Jesus Christ, I believe that you died on the cross for me. You shed your blood so that I could be forgiven and become your child. I ask the Holy Spirit to come and live inside of me. I now choose to live for you with my whole heart. I am leaving my old lifestyle and accept the Godly life you have for me. I accept your love, power and forgiveness. I not only forgive myself but those who have hurt me as well. On the cross you defeated the devil and I can have victory in my life. I love you Jesus! Amen.

If you prayed that prayer and meant it, you are now His child and you are born again. (Romans 10: 9, 10) Call someone right now and share what has just happened in your life. Find a church that teaches the whole Bible, read your Bible, pray, and start getting to know your new best friend. You are now a brand new person!! (II Cor. 5:17)

For those who have backslid
I have another confession

Spirits of Seduction
By: Kandi Rose

NOTE: This book is about my life only up to age 35 when I met the love of my life, Jesus. For three and one-half years I did not just talk the talk, I walked it. Unfortunately I let the spirit of loneliness overtake me. For the record, no man or woman is worth losing your soul and ruining your relationship with the Lord. That is what I let happen though my own choice. I met a man and ended up sleeping with him only to return to most of my sinful ways for two miserable wasted years. God kept tugging on my heart and sent so many messages and messengers my way that I made a U-Turn. I am more determined now than ever to stay on the path of holiness and take as many people with me to heaven by my testimony.

After having no peace and no more purpose in life, I finally listened once again to the voice of love calling me to return to my first love. Life had become miserable again and I missed that pure clean relationship I had once enjoyed with the love of my life, Jesus. At this time I have been, Freed by the Truth once again for almost 21 years. There's been total abstinence from all addictions. God has taken out the hard heart of hatred and has given me a soft loving heart with a definite attitude adjustment. I am not bragging on myself because self did not change me; God did. Of course I'm not perfect and my character is still being, a work in progress. I am not in intentional sin though as years past.

My passion is to see people saved and set free! If God has touched and changed your life, go and tell others. People need to hear, Jesus makes the difference! Let's brag on Jesus. The one who has set us free from, Seducing Spirits!

Spirits of Seduction
By: Kandi Rose

To purchase more books by Evangelist/Author/TV Host

Kandi Rose or to inquire about her availability to minister:

Log on www.kandiroseministries.com

Made in the USA
Middletown, DE
08 March 2019